Law Essentials

REVENUE LAW

Law Essentials

REVENUE LAW

2nd edition

William Craig, LL.B., D.I.T., M.L.I.A.

*Lecturer in Commercial Law,
Aberdeen Business School,
Robert Gordon University*

DUNDEE UNIVERSITY PRESS
2010

First edition published in Great Britain in 2007 by
Dundee University Press
University of Dundee
Dundee DD1 4HN

www.dundee.ac.uk/dup

Reprinted 2008, 2009
Second edition published 2010

ISBN 978 1 84586 103 2

No natural forests were destroyed to make this product; only farmed timber
was used and replanted.

British Library Cataloguing-in-Publication Data
A catalogue record for this book is available on request from the British Library

Typeset by Waverley Typesetters, Warham, Norfolk
Printed and bound by Bell & Bain Ltd, Glasgow

CONTENTS

TABLE OF CASES

TABLE OF STATUTES

Part 1

PRINCIPLES OF THE UK TAX SYSTEM

1 TAXATION THEORY AND THE UK SYSTEM

"In this world nothing can be said to be certain except death and taxes."

(Benjamin Franklin)

Tax has been levied on people and human activity for as long as there has been any semblance of an organised civil society. Tax has always been a contentious issue with civil unrest and wars resulting from, or motivated by, tax disputes. Tax has also been a source of sensitivity between the rulers of society, who seek to impose taxation, and those whom they seek to govern and burden with the payment of taxes. In the Roman world of two millennia ago, direct taxes were not generally levied on citizens – only on conquered territories and their peoples. Exceptional levies for specific wars or at times of crisis were charged directly to Roman citizens, but these were repaid to the people when normality was restored.[1] The key link between the benefits of being a privileged citizen, and an interaction with the finances of the state through the tax system, was important in Roman times and also included such ideas as basic social security for families from public funds.

In earlier, so-called agrarian societies, state revenues were derived mostly from non-tax sources, such as tribute, land rent and income from sovereign domains. Taxes in the proper modern sense of the word played a less significant role; only a few of them, such as land taxes or else customs and excises, contributed to state revenues on a measurable scale. This situation has changed dramatically during the last three centuries, with the advent of new industrial societies; as market and money relationships have come to dominate, taxation is the key socio-economic reality of the modern state.

PURPOSES

The primary purpose of taxation is raising revenue for government expenditure, though this need not necessarily be the purpose in order for a levy to be classified as a tax.[2] As an alternative to taxation a Government

---

[1] *Tributum*, the only direct tax levied. Taxes on sales of goods or slaves were, however, a common source of state revenue.

[2] *Northern Suburbs Cemetery Reserve Trust* v *Commonwealth* (1993), where the primary purpose of a taxing statute was to encourage employers to provide training for their staff.

might commandeer resources, increase the money supply or borrow on the market. However, taxation is either more efficient or more just than any of these. The services provided from taxation are either:

(1) services which the free market cannot provide, such as defence, law and order and public recreation facilities; or

(2) services which the state feels are better provided by itself, such as education and health (public goods).

"Social engineering" is another derivative purpose for taxation in modern societies. Purposes such as:

(1) **Redistribution of wealth**: the doctrine that tax be based on the ability to pay and that the tax system should be used to correct inequalities resulting from the impact of unregulated market forces. The degree to which these ideas have been applied varies from country to country. Currently in the UK these ideas have been given less emphasis than in the 1970s.

(2) **Management of the economy**: the notion that adjustments to tax rates have an effect on the level of economic demand and thus on the state of an economy and therefore employment, prosperity and general affluence. In recent times in the UK more emphasis has been placed on monetary measures such as interest rates and exchange rates.

(3) **Influencing behaviour**: using the tax system to influence issues of social or humanitarian importance, such as discouraging the use of alcohol and cigarettes or influencing business choices and alleviating personal impact on climate change and global warming by use of punitive taxes, tax incentives and tariff penalties.

Generally, tax is defined as a compulsory levy imposed under the law by competent state authorities for public purposes. This definition reflects certain essential elements of taxation as follows. First, taxation is not negotiable, meaning that taxation is based not on a contract, but on a compulsion. Second, taxation results in the alienation of individual property in favour of public or collective use and such alienation is possible only under the law as applied by the state. However, not all compulsory levies are taxes. Fines adjudicated by a court are not taxes; neither are individual state services such as a permit grant or a consular fee paid to the Government.

PRINCIPLES

The 18th-century Scots economist Adam Smith, in his famous work *The Wealth of Nations* (Book V, Chapter II), set out his four "canons" of taxation as follows:

(1) The subjects of every state ought to contribute towards the support of the Government, as nearly as possible, in proportion to their respective abilities; and in proportion to the revenue which they respectively enjoy under the protection of the state.

(2) The tax which each individual is bound to pay ought to be certain, and not arbitrary. The time of payment, the manner of payment, the quantity to be paid, ought all to be clear and plain to the contributor, and to every other person.

(3) Every tax ought to be levied at the time, or in the manner, in which it is most likely to be convenient for the contributor to pay it.

(4) Every tax ought to be so contrived as both to take out and keep out of the pockets of the people as little as possible over and above what it brings into the public treasury of the state.

Although, as time has passed, taxation techniques have undergone substantial revision, the principles, laid dawn by the above canons, remain surprisingly relevant. People should contribute taxes in proportion to their income and wealth, which reflects a prevailing view on distribution of tax burden. Taxes should be certain, not arbitrary; this is a principal responsibility of the Government, underlying the administration of taxes, facilitating the discharge of taxpayers' obligations and keeping costs to a reasonable minimum. There should be a balance between individual and public interests, in that taxes taken from the people should return to them in the form of the benefits of public policy or social protection. The level of compliance with Smith's ideal varies from one state to another and over any given period of time.

CLASSES OF TAXES

Taxes are numerous and various; so are the classifications of taxes. They may be classified as individual and corporate; federal and local; fixed and adjustable, etc. The basic classification is designed to distinguish between:

(1) **direct taxes**, including such classes of taxes as income taxes, capital gains taxes, property (wealth) taxes and similar taxes; and

(2) **indirect taxes**, including value added tax, excise duties and sales tax.

Direct taxes are so called because they are charged directly on persons (whether individuals or companies) in receipt (in possession) of assessable income (and similar gains) and property (wealth). By contrast, indirect taxes are charged on realisation (turnover) of assessable goods and services, and paid eventually by consumers of those goods and services; hence, other names for indirect taxes are "turnover taxes" or "taxes on consumption". This last classification, as based on "direct–indirect" criteria, encompasses all major taxes operated by leading industrial countries.

Most important of all direct taxes is income tax that accounts, on average, for up to one-third by volume of revenue raised in modern developed countries. Income tax undergoes adjustments for taxation purposes, such as the exclusion of exempted income and the addition of certain proceeds – deemed to be "income" for tax purposes only. A distinction is drawn between an income of natural persons and that of companies. Companies are said to receive "corporate profits" rather than income; thus a tax on corporate profits is mostly known as a corporate tax. Under certain conditions such differences in name may indicate more important structural differences between respective classes of taxes. For example, in the UK, corporation tax extends to cover capital gains, as a part of corporate profits. A specific capital gains tax applies exclusively to capital gains of individuals; assessable "income" of individuals would not include capital gains, unlike companies' "profits".

Worldwide, income tax is predominantly based on a global tax model, which implies uniform taxation of income, regardless of its source. In that way total income, derived by a person from all sources, is summed up and assessed at a rate that often increases proportionately with an increase in income – taxation on a progressive scale. The reason behind such progressive taxation is to make rich people, those with a higher income, pay on average more tax on each unit of their global income, than those with a lower income. There are situations when the income is taxed at a flat or even regressive rate (one that becomes lower as the income increases). Such situations are less typical, given that regressive taxation, resulting in wealth accumulation, would be contrary to social and fiscal priorities of most Governments. In reality, lower taxes tend to motivate people to report their wealth and pay at least some tax on it, which is a bargain accepted by countries with a poor tax administration and compliance record.[3]

The tax model indicated above is based on the assessment of income from all sources, globally. By contrast, a schedular tax model provides for assessment of income differently, depending on each particular source of the income. In practice the schedular tax model is rarely utilised on its own, but rather as a supplement to a global tax model, while schedular income taxation in, for example, the UK owes more to heritage than modern theory and is currently being phased out.[4]

Taxable income of individuals comprises nearly all their personal income: earnings (employment income, including benefits in kind); and non-earned income from savings and investments; income from pensions, retirement annuities, life insurance and rent; other income from land and property; and income from foreign sources. If individuals carry on business, either as self-employed persons or in partnership with others, the business income derived from such activities is part of each participant's total taxable income. As far as individuals are concerned, the computation of income tax means calculating taxable income from all sources less personal exemptions and allowances and, where appropriate, less deductions for expenses, normally those incurred in the course of deriving the income. Where a person conducts business, either on his own or in partnership, his respective income would include a business income, calculated much as for that of companies: on summing up proceeds from business and deducting allowable costs and expenses and making adjustments for losses, normally from the same business. Companies, in their turn, on computing their liability to the income (corporate) tax, must draw up a profit and loss statement, whereby they calculate profits (gross income) of their business, make adjustments for allowable expenses (costs) and losses from the business and so arrive at a net income for taxation purposes. The fact is that, save for a few countries which charge no tax on the personal income or apply a flat rate to income tax, the majority of countries worldwide (about 85 per cent) choose to assess personal income at a variable rate. Most countries distinguish between residents and non-residents, applying different criteria

---

[3] A recent example is the Russian Federation, whose tax collection record has improved considerably since the introduction in 2001 of 13% flat rate tax on an individual's income.

[4] The schedular system in the UK has a long history. In fact, when income tax was introduced in the UK in 1801, the general opinion was that a civil servant, such as a tax inspector, should not be allowed to have a full knowledge of an individual's personal income. So the income was divided into fractions to be reported to different tax inspectors under different schedules, in such a way that no single inspector might have in his hands a complete record of the taxpayer. Since then, the situation has changed radically, mostly due to membership of the EEC (EU).

to each respective category of taxpayers. Some other countries, especially those with an unsteady economy, may practise specific adjustments of the income tax rates, for example to follow rapidly moving changes to the rate of inflation.[5]

By contrast with individuals, companies are commonly taxed at a flat rate, regardless of the income volume. However, exceptions are made for certain categories of companies, especially small businesses or companies, operating in distressed regions; companies may benefit from concessions granted by the Government, in the form of a lower tax rate or even exemption from the tax on certain conditions of selective assistance or economic regeneration. Governments may also attempt to stimulate a capital inflow to their countries by granting tax concessions to foreign inward investors. There are examples of efficient tax concessions of that type, but, save for tax havens, where offering tax concessions to foreigners has become a specific national business, most other countries prefer to refrain from such practices, charging the same income tax on foreign branches as on domestic companies.

Taxation is relatively straightforward when both income receiver and taxpayer have the same "nationality", which is not always the case in the situation of a global economy. Are non-nationals deriving income from local sources liable to local tax? According to a generally accepted rule, tax residents of a country bear unlimited liability to the income tax, charged by that country ("universal tax liability"). Non-residents are liable to tax only on the income derived from local sources (limited tax liability). To distinguish between tax residents and non-residents, countries apply different criteria, most common being the "183-day stay" rule, which is the standard in the UK. The rule provides that any person staying in a particular country for 183 days or more during a year of assessment becomes a resident for taxation purposes in that country and as such bears an unlimited liability to tax, charged by the country on the taxpayer's income worldwide. Any person not caught by the "183-day stay" rule remains a non-resident for taxation purposes, with tax liability limited to the income from local sources only.[6]

For companies the residence situation is not exactly the same. Depending on a particular country, tax residence of a company would relate to either:

---

[5] In a reflection of this, the UK had to introduce an indexation allowance to modify the punitive burden of capital gains tax from 1982, as the tax up to that point taxed gains which resulted from inflation, not real increases in capital values.

[6] The "183-day stay" rule is the simplest test, which is in practice supplemented by (or even substituted with) other relevant tests, such as place of abode, permanent home, domicile, centre of vital interests etc; see further below.

(1) its place of incorporation; or

(2) a place of central management and control of the company.

Some countries, such as the USA, give preference to the first criterion; others, typically the UK, choose the second criterion; but most countries, including the UK, use a combination of both. Companies qualified as a tax resident are within tax jurisdiction of the country of their residence. This last country has a legal right to assess a worldwide income of resident companies. Moreover, even if a company does not qualify as a resident, but carries on business in the country through a specific place of business, called a "permanent establishment", such a country may charge income tax on the non-resident company insofar as the income is attributable to a permanent establishment of that company.

Since different countries may have conflicting views on tax residence, a person operating internationally runs the risk of being caught as a tax resident in more than one country and, consequently, assessed for tax more than once on the same income. Where this "double taxation" has become a real hazard, countries seek to neutralise or mitigate that hazard by granting relief from double taxation, through either exemption from further taxation of any income taxed abroad or, more commonly, a tax credit, allowing foreign taxes to be offset against the local tax on the same income. Alternatively, countries may negotiate with other interested countries as to how income taxes (and other similar taxes) should be charged in each respective country in order to avoid double taxation; this is the main role of tax treaties.

As a periodical charge, income tax is paid annually. The accounting period (a year of assessment) coincides with a calendar or fiscal year, though in some countries companies are allowed to select their own 12 months to serve as an accounting period for those companies. Within a specified period after a year of assessment (usually 3–6 months) most taxpayers (companies and often individuals) must file a return (tax declaration) with their tax inspectors to report on the taxable income. Based on those returns, tax inspectors make tax computations, or require them to be made, and assess taxpayers accordingly. Income tax is payable on financial results of a whole year of assessment; meanwhile, throughout the year, taxpayers, where required by the law, make a series of interim (advance) payments on account of a future liability to income tax, such payments, being made either monthly or quarterly, in a proportion that normally reflects income for a respective period of the previous year (or years). Deadlines, set for filing tax returns and paying taxes, must be observed. Should the taxpayer fail to comply with those deadlines without just reason, he would face heavy penalties.

The procedure of assessment and self-assessment is supplemented with a tax withholding procedure. Under this, taxpayers receive income already clear of income tax, which has been paid at source by the payer of the income, either an employer, or a bank or contracted business partner, all these taking on the responsibility of a tax agent, collecting taxes and transferring them to the tax authorities under a statutory duty imposed by law. All monies transferred in such a way are treated as a pre-paid credit against the overall amount of the income tax, due from the respective taxpayer at the end of the year of assessment.

When neither assessment nor withholding tax procedure can guarantee the collection of taxes on the income in some categories of income or of particular taxpayers, then an imputed income tax can be used. For example, tax authorities may negotiate agreements with professional associations, fixing an estimated basis for the taxation of certain professions. Members of professional associations would be subject to a simplified reporting procedure, instead of filing a standard tax return. As a rule, taxpayers are free to select between regular assessment and assessment on the basis of an imputed income. Once selection has been made, the taxpayer is discharged from further tax liability but cannot claim a refund where actual income proves to be lower than the one estimated by tax authorities' estimated or determined assessment.

Another tax within the category of direct taxes is property tax. Commonly, property tax applies to land and buildings, though, depending on a particular country, it may also reach such objects as cars, yachts, jewellery, furniture and other items of personal wealth or property of businesses. Property tax is classified as a personal wealth tax, a tax on the property (business assets) of individuals; including real estate, vehicles, computers and other items used in the course of business. As far as the property of individuals and companies is concerned, the tax may apply either to a gross value of the assessed property regardless of debts and other obligations, or, alternatively, to the net value of the asset after relevant statutory deductions. The rate of tax is flat or progressive, but the taxation threshold is usually rather high.[7] Certain items of personal property, such as household contents, personal insurance policies, works of art, some

---

[7] For example, in France taxation starts from FF 4,700,000 of personal net wealth; the rate of taxation progresses smoothly from 0.55% to the highest rate, 1.8% from FF 100,000,000 (now in Euro). The combined amount of the income and net wealth tax may not, however, exceed 85% of a net taxable income of the preceding year. Further exemptions are granted under respective treaties, concluded by France with other countries.

private collections (eg books and stamps) and the like, are usually excluded from this form of taxation.

Historically, wealth tax was common as it provided an easy source of collectable revenue on a narrow tax base. However, in modern times few countries use this method of taxation, collecting as little as 0.5–1.0 per cent on average of the total state revenue.[8] This can be contrasted with the taxation of real estate, which is now a principal source of revenue for local budgets (up to half in some states of the USA). On assessing real estate, factors such as a rental value of the property and its capital and market value are considered. Valuation of the real estate, used for personal needs, would usually differ from that of business property, and different rules apply to valuation and taxation of the land and buildings in rural and in urban areas. In general, valuation of real property for taxation purposes is a problem. In the absence of objective criteria of such evaluation, real estate has an assessable value more than is really usable to its owner. For example, the main asset owned by most individuals in the UK is a dwelling house and though it may have huge "value" and thus potential assessment "value", this is largely notional as in many cases the house is mortgaged and is the subject of punitive debt. In order to avoid possible disputes, tax authorities choose to assess the real estate at only a fraction of its real market value, which is a compromise and renders real estate taxation less effectual and constantly controversial.

There is a noticeable difference between taxes on the property itself and taxes on use and disposal of property. While property taxes apply to the value of the property, another group of taxes apply to the income, generated by the property, from its use and on disposal. Thus, a surplus of capital gives rise to capital gains tax liability upon disposal of the capital property asset. However, disposal of property without financial consideration or gain may also constitute a taxable event, relevant examples being gifts and inheritances, in which case specific gift and inheritance (estate) taxes are chargeable on transfer of the capital.

Gift taxes, as well as inheritance taxes, are structured to discriminate between taxpayers on the basis of their family relationship. Specifically, closer relatives enjoy larger exemptions from taxation, to the extent that spouses, as the closest relatives, are free from gift and inheritance (estate) tax altogether. Further exemptions may flow from social policy, aimed

---

[8] However, Switzerland has a system where wealth tax continues to play a role, with 2.5% of revenue collected by this method.

at favouring gifts to charities for educational purposes, poverty relief or religious purposes. While both taxes operate on similar principles, there remain distinctions, reflected in the structure of each particular tax. Thus, gifts, by contrast to inheritances, do not give rise to a tax liability automatically. The law may provide for so-called potentially exempted gifts, where liability to the tax is conditional upon death of the grantor within a stipulated time from the gift. Such an approach rests on a different tax treatment, as reserved in the law respectively for lifetime *inter vivos* and upon death *mortis causa* gifts. Once the gift comes within the proximity of death, that gift, though formally *inter vivos*, may constitute a death gift, to be taxed as an inheritance.[9]

Gift and inheritance (estate) taxes account for less than 1 per cent of total revenue in industrial countries, but have a more symbolic significance. With high nominal rates of taxation, its effective output is relatively low, due to numerous exemptions, deductions and allowances, mostly motivated by social and economic reasons.

Additionally, numerous problems relating to administration, including evaluation of a taxable property, prevent effective tax administration and make the yield rates low in terms of costs. The primary purpose of gift and inheritance (estate) taxes nowadays is prevention of excessive accumulation of the economic power in a few hands and, consequently, providing for more equal, and presumably fairer, distribution of national wealth: classic "social engineering".

In contrast with direct taxes, charged on property and, primarily, on income, indirect taxes are charged on a commercial turnover, that is, on transactions with certain goods and services, and, indirectly, on consumers of those goods and services, who become, therefore, eventual payers of the tax. The most important among indirect taxes is value added tax (VAT), which has steadily increased in importance in modern consumption-based societies, presently raising nearly as much revenue as income tax and more than any other indirect tax. VAT is a universal turnover tax and applies to all goods and services save for certain exceptions. The tax is designed to be charged on each accretion in the value of assessable goods and services, realised at every stage of a production and distribution process, to ensure that the total tax collected at all stages of the process is the same as if it were charged once on the highest value of respective goods and services. To that end, the system operates a "credit" formula of computation of the VAT payable at any stage, as follows:

---

[9] See the Inheritance Tax Act 1984 (UK), which has a 7-year rule to this effect to prevent deathbed transfers in order to avoid tax.

(1) output tax, collected on sale of the goods and services, less credit for the amount of

(2) input tax, paid on purchase of the same goods and services,

(3) the difference, normally positive, being payable to tax authorities;

(4) any VAT paid on purchased goods (services) that cannot be recovered as above is written off as a cost.

Historically, turnover taxes were charged on a cumulative basis, that is, in full amount at each stage, which tended to be excessive as a burden to those paying the tax. France produced a workable solution to this problem in turnover taxes, with the concept of a "value added tax" in 1954 which formed the basis for the EEC, the forerunner of the European Union. Nowadays, the VAT system is operated by more than 50 countries, among them most of the industrially developed countries, with the exception of the USA, where only one state – Michigan – has its version of VAT. Adoption of the value added tax is a precondition of membership of the European Union. The Union has contributed much to unification of indirect taxes in its member countries, by promoting a system of VAT, which tax is also a principal revenue raiser for the Union, since as much as 1.4 per cent of the VAT of member countries is presently accumulated in the Union budget.

In order to regulate a tax burden, falling on consumers of respective categories of goods and services, VAT is charged at a gradated rate. Standard-rate tax applies to the majority of taxable transactions, whereas a lower rate is usually charged on transactions involving basic goods and services, such as foodstuffs, medicines and public utilities. Some goods and services are exempt from VAT; others are taxed at a zero rate, which renders such goods less expensive because of their social value without excluding them from the VAT credit system. When goods and services are exempt from VAT, suppliers may not claim a refund (credit) for the input tax on such items. The administration of VAT has some specific problems because of the complexity of the movement of goods and services, and effective tax administration in VAT depends on a continuous control over all stages of the commercial chain. In the absence of such control, turnover may easily escape taxation. Tax control entails additional administrative costs and, unless a certain threshold is reached, there seems to be little economic sense in attempting the tax collection, as costs, incurred in the process, exceed revenue raised. Hence, a minimum value exemption for VAT purposes has become common practice in most countries.

Another turnover tax which, though extremely prevalent in the past, has nowadays lost much of its importance, is excise duty. In contrast with

VAT, excise duty applies exclusively to specific categories of goods, such as salt, tobacco, spirits, wine and beer etc, traditionally covered by a state fiscal monopoly, or, alternatively, to oil and gas, luxury goods and other goods that are usually subject to extra taxation. Whereas VAT, by the nature of its operation, is a multi-stage tax, excise duties apply only once and on the whole turnover of taxable goods, at such a stage of the manufacture and distribution process as may be specified by the fiscal authorities. It is common to charge excise duties in fixed amounts on each physical unit of the goods (for example, spirits are assessed on their alcohol contents), though *ad valorem* assessment is used, where appropriate, for example, on charging an excise on jewellery and other luxury goods. Customs duties are an indirect tax, levied on cross-border transactions involving certain specified goods, the charge playing an essential regulatory role, and Governments often use such a tax to promote exports or to protect the domestic market from undesirable imports.[10]

As some countries may operate their own turnover taxes, conceptually different from those described above, we should not omit reference to sales taxes. Sales taxes combine elements of both VAT and excise duty but in their own way. Similar to VAT, sales taxes are universal, as they cover most goods and services. But unlike VAT, which reaches all stages of the manufacture and distribution of taxable goods and services, sales taxes are focused on retail sales of taxable goods and services and do not usually apply beyond those limits. Accordingly, sales taxes are charged in a lump sum, never fall into fractions and are similar to traditional turnover taxes such as excises. In the USA, they are imposed at the state level, where they account for one-third of the revenue base overall but are not applied in all states and not in any uniform pattern in states where they are applied. Most other industrial countries give preference to VAT as a recognised alternative to sales taxes and only Canada and the Russian Federation charge both VAT and sales tax at the same time.

TAXATION LAW ENFORCEMENT AND COMPLIANCE

Taxation law regulates relations between the Government and private persons and thus falls within the domain of public law, and relates to state sovereignty. This means that most obligations arising from taxation

---

[10] Presently, this practice is mostly unified by the General Agreement on Tariffs and Trade (GATT) and other relevant international Conventions, so that countries are not completely free in the regulative use of customs duties, if not within the limits, as prescribed by the above documents.

law, unlike contracts between private persons, bind taxpayers without reciprocity on the part of the Government. Taxation law deals primarily with domestic affairs, though, as far as taxation of international activities is concerned, special procedures, relating to the international taxation law, serve to supplement domestic law of particular countries, to safeguard against double taxation of business or personal activity.

The key elements of taxation are as follows:

(1) Liability to pay tax accrues to a taxpayer as specified by law.

(2) Taxation has an object, namely income, or property, or transaction, or any other fact and event, which according to the law gives rise to taxation ("taxable event").

(3) Tax applies to a tax base, being a value of the taxation object or, alternatively, any other characteristic of the same, taken as a "base for assessment".

(4) Tax is charged *pro rata* on the tax base, alternatively, in a specific amount on each unit of the tax base.

(5) To determine the tax, computation rules designed for the purpose are used.

(6) Tax is payable with reference to a tax period, in a way and within time limits as prescribed by law.

The law operates to validate taxes. For a tax to be legally imposed it must be set under law-making procedure and must be formally put into operation from a certain date. Where prescribed by law, taxpayers must report on their business and employment activities for taxation purposes. Such procedures, known in the UK currently as self-assessment, provide for filing a tax return, whereby taxpayers disclose information on their income, property and other relevant information.

The law prescribes how and when taxes must be paid. Should a taxpayer fail to pay any tax, he becomes exposed to tax enforcement procedure. Tax authorities enjoy extensive powers to this effect. In case of taxpayers' non-compliance with taxation rules, tax authorities are entitled to charge interest, where the tax payment is overdue, or fines, or both penalties at the same time, as appropriate. Such civil penalties apply to less serious offences, resulting through negligence, rather than intention; however, where more specific and serious intentional breach of taxation rules takes place, criminal charges may be brought.

Whichever penalties are charged on taxpayers, they have a right to appeal. Usually, the taxpayer who is not satisfied with the assessment of his tax affairs, files a complaint that goes under an administrative procedure from lower to higher tax management level, and only if no satisfaction is obtained there may the taxpayer expect his case to be tried by a competent court. The established practice of trying tax disputes in dedicated tribunals reflects the fact that tax disputes are of a highly technical nature and require, therefore, particular expertise on the part of the court. Participation of independent tax professionals in proceedings will decide tax disputes more effectively, at least on their technical facts, with the potential for them to be challenged in a court of general jurisdiction, usually only on questions of law.

On the adoption of the Bill of Rights in 1688, England (and by implication the whole of the UK) was the first to subscribe to the fundamental principle of taxation law, providing that taxes cannot be imposed save by consent of Parliament. For most countries nowadays, primary legislation (rules, passed by the Parliament, as distinct from delegated legislation, passed by executive bodies within legislative powers, conferred on them by the Parliament) forms the major source of taxation law.[11] Such legislation comprises consolidation acts and specific tax legislation and Finance Acts, adopted at regular intervals, usually each year, providing for the operation of the tax system. The trend is to make primary legislation as comprehensive as practicable and to reduce application of the delegated legislation to a reasonable minimum so as to retain better control over taxation law from the perspective of human rights.

Tax authorities are competent to issue guidance assisting taxpayers in the practical issues concerning the operation of taxation law, examples being statements of practice, Revenue rulings, instruction manuals and other materials issued by tax authorities for this purpose. Exceptionally, the law may confer on tax authorities power to revise faulty procedures and repair gaps in the law through so-called "extra-statutory concessions". However, tax authorities are usually limited to the interpretation of taxation law within rather rigorous restrictions. Such limitations serve to prevent "law-making" on the part of the tax authorities, without the authority of Parliament or the sanction of the courts.

Essential Facts

- The primary purpose of taxation is raising revenue for government expenditure.

---

[11] However, under the devolution settlement in the UK for Scotland, the Scottish Parliament has extensive tax-raising and varying powers: Scotland Act 1998.

- "Social engineering" is one derivation purpose of taxation, through redistribution of wealth, management of the economy and influencing consumer behaviour.
- Tax is defined as a compulsory levy imposed under the law by competent state authorities for public purposes.
- Adam Smith set out four "canons" of taxation, relating to ability to pay; certainty of requirements; timing of levy; and balancing of individual and public interests.
- Taxes may be classified as direct or indirect.
- Most obligations arising from taxation law bind taxpayers without reciprocity on the part of the Government. Enforcement and compliance rules may be laid down by law, with penalties attaching to taxpayers who fail to observe them.

2 THE EUROPEAN DIMENSION

Where disputes on tax matters arise between private persons, or Governments and intergovernmental organisations, such disputes usually start and end up in domestic courts. Exceptions are the EU courts (European Court of Justice and the Court of First Instance). These last courts, as judicial institutions of the EU, bear their share of responsibility for the European legal order, and as such are competent to try actions, brought by private persons against European Governments and other official institutions, for any breach of the EU law, for example for failure to repeal such a domestic tax that has been outlawed in the Union. As EU law deals with taxation issues of member countries, appeal from domestic courts on questions of European law, relating to those issues, would go to the ECJ for decision. Decisions, once made, become binding upon parties to the dispute and enforceable through regular procedures accordingly. However, the fact remains that the situation within the European Union is unique in many substantial aspects, given that the Union, unlike most other intergovernmental organisations and alliances, has been endowed with supranational powers by its underlying treaties. The Union generates dedicated legislation, which has a direct effect and supremacy over the whole territory of the EU – now some 27 nation states. The law is operated by the EU courts (ECJ and ECHR)[1] that exercise functions and responsibilities within the Union similar to domestic courts of the EU member countries within their national territory.

CONFLICT OF LAWS

Integration of the law is based on respective obligations of the member countries under the EC Treaty. Save for such obligations, and the relatively novel procedure laid down in the EU Arbitration Convention,[2] countries would decide any tax dispute exclusively on application of domestic regulations and judicial procedures. When, therefore, a dispute arises on tax matters between foreign nationals and their state of domicile and residence, the domestic courts normally decline to rule on such a dispute as *forum non conveniens*. The courts will not enforce a foreign tax

---

[1] European Court of Justice and European Court of Human Rights.
[2] 90/436/EEC 2004.

law, as a rule. At the same time, the courts recognise a taxation law of other countries, so they may refuse to give effect on their territory to any contract or transaction that expressly violates a foreign law.

One may appreciate the conditional character of "illegality" on the following examples from the practice of English courts. In *Re Emery's Investment Trusts* (1959) a husband, hoping to avoid payment of a US federal tax, bought certain American securities in his wife's name. Later, when the wife refused him a share in the proceeds from resale of the securities, the husband attempted to reverse the contractual arrangements for the holding of the securities, and by so doing had to disclose his actual motives in the purchase, namely avoiding a foreign tax. Since the only possibility of rebutting a presumption of advancement was to adduce an evidence of illegal motive (defrauding foreign tax authorities), the court did not accept such evidence, and decided against the claimant.

In another case, *Euro-Diam Ltd* v *Bathurst* (1987), however, the outcome was different. The claimant, an English company, contracted for delivery of diamonds to a German customer. At the request of the latter, seeking to save money on German custom duties, the price as shown in delivery documents was only half the actual price for the diamonds. The delivery was insured with an English company, under English law. Unfortunately, the diamonds were stolen, so a claim was brought against the insurers for recovery of the actual value of the stolen diamonds. The insurers, however, sought to avoid liability, pleading that the insurance contract was tainted with illegality, and as such unenforceable in the English court. The court refused to accept that argument as the illegality only derived from a foreign tax law, and, under the English law, the insurance contract was perfectly legal and binding upon the parties. The claimant, therefore, had a good title to recover irrespective of any third party rights. Why the difference? Whereas, in the first case, the claimant must have cited his illegal conduct to uphold his claim under the English law, in the second case the claim was presumed to be valid under English law – the presumption was not rebutted by reference to a foreign tax law, as this was deemed irrelevant by the court.

ASPECTS OF EU LAW RELEVANT TO INTERNATIONAL TAX PLANNING

The Treaty of Rome 1957 (EC Treaty) assigns to the EC Commission the task, in consultation with the Member States, of eliminating distortions in competition caused by differences in the law and administrative practices of those States, in order to establish and maintain a common market.

This is most clearly laid down in Art 3 of the Treaty, which provides as follows:

> "(1) For the purposes set out in Article 2, the activities of the Community shall include: ...
>
> (c) an internal market characterised by the abolition, as between Member States, of obstacles to the free movement of goods, persons, services and capital; ...
>
> (g) a system ensuring that competition in the internal market is not distorted;
>
> (h) the approximation of the laws of Member States to the extent required for the functioning of the common market."

The result has been many initiatives to co-ordinate or harmonise Member State legislation, including tax law. Accordingly, the European legislator has been active in taking measures regarding both direct and indirect taxation. However, it should be noted that no provision in the EC Treaty refers to taxes, except the following:

- Arts 90–95, dealing with harmonisation of taxes and the prohibition of discrimination in tax matters;
- Art 293, dealing with, among other things, the prohibition of double taxation; and
- Art 58, dealing with the treatment of resident and non-resident taxpayers.

Article 58 is important as it deals with the treatment of resident and non-resident taxpayers and it reads as follows:

> "(1) The provisions of Article 56 n[2] shall be without prejudice to the right of Member States:
>
> (a) to apply the relevant provisions of their tax law, which distinguish between taxpayers who are not in the same situation with regard to their place of residence or with regard to the place where their capital is invested;
>
> (b) to take all requisite measures to prevent infringements of national law and regulations, in particular in the field of taxation and the prudential supervision of financial institutions, or to lay down procedures for the declaration of capital movements for purposes of administrative or statistical information, or to take measures which are justified on grounds of public policy or public security.

(2) The provisions of this chapter shall be without prejudice to the applicability of restrictions on the right of establishment which are compatible with this Treaty.

(3) The measures and procedures referred to in paragraphs 1 and 2 shall not constitute a means of arbitrary discrimination or a disguised restriction on the free movement of capital and payments as defined in Article 56."

Another important principle of EU law, which may be essential in the area of taxation, is the provision contained in Art 12 of the EC Treaty (the non-discrimination principle). Article 12 reads as follows: "Within the scope of application of this Treaty, and without prejudice to any special provisions contained therein, any discrimination on grounds of nationality shall be prohibited."

The provision makes clear that the non-discrimination principle under EU law is based only on nationality. Any person who has the nationality of one of the Member States may, within the scope of the EC Treaty, not be treated worse than a person who has the nationality of another Member State. This provision is the basis of interpretation of the "Four Freedoms", which will be discussed in further detail below.

THE EU CONCEPTS OF FREEDOM AND DISCRIMINATION

Non-discrimination provisions in the area of international tax are aimed at preventing discrimination based on nationality. Nationals of one State may not, if placed in the same situation, be less favourably treated in the other State than nationals of that State. This principle is included in Art 24 of the Organisation for Economic Co-operation and Development (OECD) and UN Model Treaties, almost all bilateral tax treaties and in Art 12 of the EC Treaty.

As discussed above, Art 2 of the EC Treaty provides that the task of the EC is, among other things, to establish an internal (common) market and an economic and monetary union. According to the European Court of Justice (ECJ), the internal market entails "the elimination of all obstacles to intra-Community trade in order to merge the national markets into a single market bringing about conditions as close as possible to those of a genuine Internal Market".

As mentioned above, Art 3 of the EC Treaty specifies a number of features of an internal market (the "Four Freedoms"), including the following:

- the abolition between the Member States of all obstacles to the free movement of goods, persons, services and capital (Art 3(c)); and
- the approximation of laws of the Member States (Art 3(h)).

The "Four Freedoms" encompass two principles: (1) the right of cross-border circulation throughout the EU; and (2) the prohibition of discrimination on the grounds of nationality and origin.

The free movement of goods is implemented in more detail in Arts 23–38 of the EC Treaty. It refers mainly to the abolition of all tariff barriers at the border (ie prohibition of customs duties and similar charges) and all non-tariff barriers at the border, quantitative restrictions on imports and other similar restrictions. The free movement of persons is broken down into two components: (1) the free movement of workers (Arts 39–42 of the EC Treaty); and (2) the freedom of establishment (Arts 43–48 of the EC Treaty).

(1) Free movement of workers

The free movement of workers encompasses the following:

- the freedom of migration, the right to accept employment abroad, the right to leave one's Member State or country of origin, the right to enter another Member State and the right to live in that other Member State; and
- a prohibition of discrimination, a prohibition of different treatment of workers from other Member States in respect of employment, remuneration and working conditions.

The free movement of persons is subject to limitations justified on grounds of public policy, public security or public health. If none of these limitations applies, the concept entails the right:

- to offer or accept employment made throughout the EU;
- to move freely throughout the EU for this purpose;
- to residence in a Member State for the purpose of employment in accordance with the provisions governing the employment of nationals of that State; and
- to residence in the territory of a Member State after having been employed in that State.

(2) Freedom of establishment

The freedom of establishment includes:

- the right to take up and carry on activities as a self-employed person and to set up and manage undertakings; and
- the right to equal treatment in the Member States involved.

The right of freedom of establishment is conferred upon both individuals having the nationality of an EU Member State and legal entities having their registered office, central administration or principal place of business within the EC. The right encompasses both the right to set up a new business (primary establishment) and the right to set up agencies, branches and subsidiaries of existing undertakings (secondary establishment).

(3) Freedom of capital

A third pillar of the principle of freedom to move throughout the EU is the freedom of capital. Enterprises must be free to borrow money or to issue shares where, in their opinion, the cost of capital is lowest. Investors must be free to invest their money where they feel the risk/yield ratio is best. Therefore, the EC Treaty also ensures the freedom of capital, as well as the freedom of payments. In fact, the freedom of payments is complementary to the other "Four Freedoms". For example, the freedom of workers is of little use to a frontier worker if he is unable to transfer his wages home from his country of employment.

(4) Freedom of services

The freedom of services can be distinguished from the free movement of goods in that services are intangible. It is also complementary to the other freedoms. However, it is needed as a separate category, because cross-border provision of services may well take place without goods being moved and without secondary establishments across the border. The freedom to provide services encompasses a right, for the service provider, to enter and to sojourn and a right to be treated in the same manner as nationals.

In a series of decisions issued since 1986,[3] the ECJ has interpreted the scope and importance of these "Four Freedoms" in practice. In doing so, it has also outlined the criteria and conditions with which domestic laws of the Member States should comply, in order not to violate the principles laid down in the "Four Freedoms".

---

[3] See, for example, among others: *Commission* v *France* (1986); *ICI* v *Colmer* (1996); *Gervais Larsy* v *INASTI* (2001); *Schumacher* (1995); *Gebhard* (1996); *Compagnie de Saint-Gobain* (2000); *Royal Bank of Scotland plc* v *Greek State* (1999); *Verkooijen* (2000); *De Lasteyrie* (2004), and *Marks & Spencer* (2005).

Taken together, the "Four Freedoms" basically cover all forms of cross-border activity and investment within the European Union. Their scope is twofold:

(1) they prohibit rules entailing discriminatory restrictions on the exercise of the freedoms, national rules, which discriminate either directly or indirectly on the grounds of nationality;

(2) the EC Treaty also prohibits certain non-discriminatory restrictions, restrictions which do not entail discrimination, but nonetheless place cross-border activity at a disadvantage.

There is a good amount of literature about the differences between discriminatory and non-discriminatory restrictions; but for most practical purposes it is sufficient to ask two basic questions:

(i) Is the exercise of a Treaty freedom disadvantaged?

The question as to whether the exercise of an EC Treaty freedom is disadvantaged can perhaps be best illustrated by an example:

Is a person who is investing or carrying on an activity across a border within the EU placed at a disadvantage by a Member State? In the tax area the disadvantage could, for instance, take the form of:

– a higher tax rate;

– the refusal of a relief; or

– the imposition of a more onerous procedural requirement.

If the answer to the first question is that a disadvantage exists, the onus is then on the Member State to show that the disadvantage is justified.

(ii) What justifications are acceptable?

In fact, Member States have been conspicuously unsuccessful in persuading the court to accept the justifications they have put forward.

From the above, it follows that there are three kinds of national measures that are "suspect" from the point of view of the "Four Freedoms". They are:

(1) measures overtly making a distinction on the basis of nationality or origin;

(2) measures indirectly putting products, capital or economic operators of other Member States at a disadvantage, eg a distinction between resident and non-resident taxpayers on the basis of a criterion

which, as such, is irrelevant for taxation purposes and mainly affects nationals of other Member States; or

(3) measures without distinction, but which restrict intra-EC trade or movement of capital.

Some defences put forward by Member States as a justification for discriminatory treatment or for a restriction of one of the "Four freedoms" have been rejected by the ECJ, including the following:

- absence of harmonisation;

- avoidance of discrimination;

- economic aims;

- protection of tax revenue;

- absence of reciprocity; and

- administrative difficulties.

EU LAW IN GENERAL

The courts in EC law adopt a fully purposive approach to legal interpretation, such that the principles work down to be applied to the facts and thus literal interpretations are rejected in favour of seeking the purpose of the Directive or other matter of law. This can cause difficulties with UK law in implementation of EU Directives and in the attitude by the UK establishment to certain seemingly controversial ECJ decisions. Abuse of right is a well-developed concept in many European civil law systems and has come to be applied by the ECJ to rules of EC law and thus applicable to the domestic law of all Member States including non-civil law states such as the UK. In its recent application by the ECJ, at the instigation of HMRC,[4] to strike down VAT tax avoidance arrangements made by a series of UK companies as being abusive and not consistent with an economic activity in the Single Market,[5] it proved equally controversial. UK institutions almost instinctively resist the importation of a foreign legal style or principle to our jurisprudence; even when it is eminently equitable. This is another echo of the most fundamental of tax issues: sovereignty.

---

[4] Her Majesty's Revenue & Customs.
[5] *Halifax/BUPA/University of Huddersfield* (2005).

Essential Facts

- The European Court of Justice and the Court of First Instance are competent to try actions, brought by private persons against European Governments and other official institutions, for any break of the EU law regarding taxation.
- Integration of the law is based on the respective obligations of the member countries under the EC Treaty.
- The EC Commission is charged with eliminating distortions in competition caused by differences in the law and administrative practices of the Member States.
- The concepts of freedom of movement of goods, persons, services and capital and of non-discrimination are protected by EC and taxation treaties.
- The application of the purposive approach to legal interpretation reflects the fundamental taxation issue of sovereignty.

3 INTERNATIONAL TAXATION AND THE TAX TREATY SYSTEM

THEORY AND BACKGROUND

National tax systems are drawn up with the interests of that sovereign nation, and not primarily with the interests of other jurisdictions, in mind. Whenever different countries interact in the taxation sphere, the problem of conflict of tax jurisdiction arises. Countries establish their jurisdiction over tax matters unilaterally, or in agreement with another country or countries. As taxable profits or gains arise from sources in more than one country, taxation of such profits or gains might duplicate action in another jurisdiction. This problem of "double taxation" is normally remedied by specific domestic legislation and international tax treaties. Tax treaties are concluded between two or more countries with a primary purpose of eliminating double taxation, while providing for administrative and legal assistance and information exchange on tax matters. Still closer co-ordination has been achieved within the European Union, where taxation policies of member countries are centrally regulated in some essential aspects as outlined in the Chapter 2.[1]

Co-ordination of tax jurisdiction is a particular concern of the international tax law system which has two distinct aspects:

(1) domestic tax law as it applies to non-residents, on taxable profits or gains from domestic sources, and residents on their taxable profits or gains worldwide; and

(2) tax treaties, primarily treaties on avoidance of double taxation domestically and worldwide.

Both of the above layers of international law are interconnected, though each of them contributes to the body of law in its own right. For a rule to become binding upon any particular country, that jurisdiction must have consented to it.[2]

---

[1] Article 93 of the European Community Treaty provides for harmonisation of "turnover" taxes in the EC. In 1967 First VAT Directive (Directive 27/227) laid down principles of the European VAT. Details were added by the Second Directive. This last was replaced in 1977, with the Sixth VAT Directive (Directive 77/388) (as amended and extended) now in force.

[2] *Govt of India* v *Taylor* (1955); where the issues of national sovereignty and consent to enforcement of foreign jurisdictions were explored.

SOURCES OF INTERNATIONAL TAX LAW

Tax law does not traditionally form part of what is called private international law; however, international co-operation has developed through international institutions such as the OECD, the UN and the EU. The limited sources of law, such as they exist, specifically related to international taxation issues can be found in particular in the Statute of the International Court of Justice. According to Art 38(1) of that Statute, the Court, on deciding upon disputes submitted to it, shall consider the following sources:

(a) international Conventions, whether general or particular, establishing rules expressly recognised by the contesting states;

(b) international custom, as evidence of a general practice accepted as law;

(c) the general principles of law recognised by civilised nations;

(d) judicial decisions and the writings of the most highly regarded academics and jurists of various nations, as a subsidiary path for the determination of legal rules.

Some of the sources of international law are presumed to have priority over other sources, so that the above list presents a hierarchy of the sources in applying international law. Of most importance are Conventions and treaties, legally binding upon signatories to these Conventions and treaties. The validity of international agreements as a primary source of international law flows from the fact that countries, clearly and unambiguously undertake to abide by certain rules in relation to other countries and allow these rules to be enforceable against them within certain international arbitration procedures. Furthermore, international agreements are governed by long-established customary rules and standards, of which the most important have undergone codification in the Vienna Convention on the Law of Treaties.[3]

It should be mentioned that international agreements, including those on tax matters, commonly prevail over municipal law.[4] Respective provisions are found in the constitutions and other legislation of most

---

[3] In force since 1980.

[4] Certain law systems might have different interpretations as to whether international agreements always prevail over their domestic law. Some countries apply the doctrine *lex posterior derogat legi priori* to retain a right to adopt a new law in substitution for any existing law, including international agreements. Other countries apply the doctrine *lex specialis* to amend the effects of international agreements by introducing specific regulations, which in this case are said to have priority over more general regulations, provided by relevant international agreements.

countries. As international co-operation continues to expand, so international law becomes an increasingly important element of domestic law systems, revolutionising application in some substantial aspects. The United Kingdom evidences this trend as follows:

- According to the Bill of Rights of 1688 no taxes can be imposed save by consent of Parliament. Since then, Parliament has been exercising its exclusive authority in tax matters. *If there is no authority of Parliament, there is no liability to tax.* That rule was a pillar of the UK tax system for centuries. Nowadays, however, UK taxes have become more conditional on international obligations. As a member of the European Union, the country must abide by the EU treaties, Regulations and Directives. The EC Treaty, to which the UK has been a party since 1973, has immediate effect in all Member States without further enactment by parliaments.
- No parliamentary consent is formally needed to give effect in the UK to EU law, in particular on custom duties and value added tax, introduced by Regulations and Directives, outside direct control of the UK Parliament. Furthermore, the UK Government has concluded more than 100 double taxation treaties with other countries. Those treaties, purporting to substitute the domestic tax regime with a specific one negotiated for the purpose with a treaty partner, are given effect as Orders in Council, again without a specific enactment by Parliament. Though commentators argue that such treaties remain secondary to the UK law and may be repealed by Parliament, where appropriate, the situation is that the international law overrides *de facto* the UK domestic law, sometimes in breach of fundamental national traditions. This is the price the UK pays for closer integration and co-operation in tax matters with its trading partners.

TAX TREATIES

Much of the focus in this area of tax law is on the prevention of "double taxation", hence the tendency among law practitioners in this area to highlight the role of the OECD Model.[5] There are, in addition to this, many other bilateral and multilateral agreements which have relevance to tax disputes:

- the European Convention on Human Rights;
- the EC Treaty;

---

[5] OECD Model Convention on the Prevention of Double Taxation.

- the Vienna Convention on the Law of Treaties;
- social security treaties;
- general treaties on mutual assistance and information exchange;
- other bilateral tax treaties and ancillary Conventions governing specific taxes or specific situations.

The legal effect of any such treaties will vary from country to country and will be dependent on the constitutional make-up of the particular sovereign state. There are three methods by which treaties can become active in a state:

(1) *automatic integration model*: where treaties become law upon signing – this applies, for example, in France, Spain and Switzerland;

(2) *formal incorporation model*: where treaties require an executive or legislative act to formally bring them into force – this applies in Germany and the USA;

(3) *substantive incorporation*: where a special enactment is required and the treaty has no effect in domestic law of itself, thus careful scrutiny is needed to see the actual domestic effect of each individual treaty – this applies in Australia, Canada and the UK.

In some countries, most notably France, a treaty entered into by the state is constitutionally superior to domestic law and thus no conflict can arise. However, in the majority of states from all three models of incorporation, treaties hold equivalent status to domestic laws and can thus be selectively overridden by subsequent legislation. Override is uncertain in most jurisdictions as it runs contrary to the basic principle of international law,[6] and even where allowed it may be for the courts to ascertain whether a legislature actually intended to override a treaty obligation in making a new domestic law.[7]

INTERPRETATION

Treaty interpretation is in the realm of conflict of laws and involves legal tradition and method, both generally and specific to taxation. One must consider the attitude of the courts generally in the relevant jurisdiction, and the attitude to the particular treaty in question with its specific content, and the role of the Vienna Convention[8] both of itself and in

---

[6] *Pacta sunt servanda* (agreements must be kept).

[7] See generally for an expert view of this area, B Conforti, *International Law and the Role of Domestic Legal Systems*.

[8] Vienna Convention on the Law of Treaties.

allowing possible consultation of relevant supplementary material.[9] It is in a synthesis of these several strands of variable that we view court decisions in various jurisdictions on the interpretation of tax treaties.

It is a desirable goal for tax treaties to be commonly interpreted by the courts of both parties to the treaty and using the same methodology. This is most closely achieved in the Commentary to the OECD Treaty,[10] hence its popularity as an aid in interpreting tax treaties generally and as a useful contributor to international co-operation. It is also desirable that each jurisdiction take note of the tax decisions of others, and this is evidenced in the growing practice of citing tax treaty interpretation from the jurisprudence of other countries.[11]

The OECD Model has now become the standard for the drafting of tax treaties, but it is not a template for a uniform treaty. In each negotiation between prospective parties to a new treaty the peculiarities of each of the domestic tax systems and the domestic legal systems generally must be foremost. Many countries have their own methods or model which, while adopting aspects of the OECD Model, mark them out as distinctive in their own right. The USA, for example, has in modern times placed great emphasis on anti-treaty-shopping measures; it also includes its policy on taxing its citizens wherever they reside in the world, and respects the individual autonomy of its constituent states.

In contrast to the OECD Model and its influence, many developing countries follow the UN Model[12] as it is designed to assist the interests of such countries, and OECD members tend to accommodate this desire. It is now recognised that there are problems with the existing bilateral treaty network, largely caused by the complexities of global trade and the speed of transaction imposed by new technologies,[13] and thus the expansion and improvement of the treaty network will require a multilateral approach in the future.

JUDICIAL PRACTICE AND ENFORCEMENT

The hierarchy of sources of international law has an impact on judicial practice both domestically and internationally. The key question for domestic courts on application of the international law is whether this law

---

[9] For an expert consideration of these complex issues, see P Baker, *Double Taxation Conventions* (2001).

[10] See www.OECD.org.

[11] See *Thiel v Commissioner for Taxation* (1990).

[12] United Nations Model Double Taxation Convention Between Developed and Developing Countries (2001).

[13] See, generally, W J Craig, *Taxation of E-Commerce* (2nd edn, 2001).

has been received into respective domestic legislation. For treaties, which require ratification, reception into domestic legislation and their subsequent application by domestic courts would depend on the ratification conditions being satisfied. In the case of a customary practice, its recognition as a source of international law is normally conditional on a legal qualification, and also on other factors: where some countries automatically adopt qualified international customs, unless they prove inconsistent with domestic legislation, other countries require "naturalisation" of the international custom by a distinct legislative action, judicial decision or established local usage. International tribunals treat domestic legislation as a question of established fact, taken in a specific context of the relevant international law.

Any international disputes on tax matters are settled mostly under a standard judicial procedure.[14] Parties must attempt to negotiate on the disputed issue prior to any judicial proceedings. Should no satisfaction be obtained through negotiations, different options, depending on the status of the litigants and the nature of their dispute, are possible. Where litigants are states and intergovernmental organisations, disputes between such parties may be referred for consideration to international tribunals with the relevant competence. Under the auspices of the General Agreement on Tariffs and Trade (GATT), for example, there are *ad hoc* tribunals, known as "Dispute Settlement Panels", convened by the WTO General Council (its Dispute Settlement Body) for trying specific cases, related to implementation of the GATT by participants to this agreement. Another example is the European Court of Justice, competent to try disputes arising out of the EU treaties and Directives and secondary legislation on tax matters. Decisions that are taken by such international tribunals have a binding effect on parties to the dispute. Enforcement of such decisions, with regard to a sovereign status of the parties concerned, is carried out within the procedures provided by respective international agreements and sponsoring organisations.

ARBITRATION IN INTERNATIONAL TAX DISPUTE RESOLUTION

Most bilateral tax Conventions provide for a mutual agreement procedure as a means of resolving disputes concerning the application of the Convention to taxpayers. This procedure entails discussions between the competent authorities of the two signatory states.

---

[14] See the EU Arbitration Convention, eg (90/436/EEC 2004).

The competent authority procedure has provided many benefits to international business and is widely accepted as the best method of resolving instances of double taxation. However, this process presents certain imperfections.

- Double taxation Conventions generally encourage, but do not require, the competent authorities to eliminate double taxation. It is, therefore, possible that double taxation will remain after the mutual agreement procedure has been applied.

- The affected taxpayers are normally excluded from the competent authority deliberations or, in any event, have no official or guaranteed status in such deliberations.

- Double taxation Conventions establish no procedural rules or time limits for competent authority proceedings, and specify no method for their implementation (although many Conventions stipulate that competent authority agreements will be implemented notwithstanding national time limits).

- There are numerous procedural conflicts between competent authority and domestic examination and appeal rules.

- Delays in reaching a conclusion of competent authority proceedings can be very long, and are of concern to businesses.

Binding and compulsory arbitration can eliminate or alleviate many of these concerns. Arbitration always reaches a conclusion, provides for impartial determinations with proper taxpayer participation, and applies law to resolve the dispute. While arbitration may also present delays, the process is orderly, predictable and transparent.

CURRENT USE OF ARBITRATION

There has been an important, albeit limited expansion in the use of arbitration in international taxation in recent times with two developments in particular:

The EU Convention

In 1990, the states of the then European Community concluded a Convention providing for the use of arbitration in certain international taxation disputes (the EU Convention). This Convention represents an important precedent which merits consideration in framing the appropriate terms for international arbitration provisions in general. The following characteristics of the EU Convention should be noted:

- It is a multilateral agreement.
- Arbitration is compulsory.
- The result of the arbitration is not technically binding, but the Convention does ensure that a binding result is obtained. Following an arbitration decision, the competent authorities are provided with an opportunity to achieve an alternative resolution, but it must be one which eliminates double taxation.
- The Convention applies to permanent establishments as well as companies.
- It applies to both juridical and economic double taxation. However, only those cases of double taxation arising from adjustments under Art 9 (Associated Enterprises) of the OECD Model Tax Convention on Income and Capital (the OECD Model Convention) are covered.
- The taxpayer has the right to initiate arbitration ("right of initiative").
- The Convention establishes a timetable: the enterprise has 3 years to present the case to arbitration; the competent authorities have 2 years to resolve the matter under the mutual agreement procedure; if this does not occur, the competent authorities have 6 months to establish an "advisory commission", which commission has 6 months to decide the case.
- No rules of procedure are prescribed. These are to be determined by the competent authorities.
- No judicial review is permitted.
- Arbitration is not applicable in cases of "serious penalty."
- Arbitration decisions must be implemented regardless of any domestic time limits. Such implementation may be by adjusting income or providing a tax credit.

Several aspects of the EU Convention could be adapted for use between various states in advancing the international arbitration of tax disputes. For example, the EU Convention demonstrates that a multilateral Convention is a realistic alternative to the adoption of arbitration clauses in bilateral Conventions. The combination of arbitration and competent authority action in the EU Convention is interesting, and does ensure that double taxation is avoided, but not necessarily in accordance with legal principles or in a manner which is fair to the taxpayer, and this represents an area where improvement is required.

Transfer pricing issues are likely to be the primary focus of international arbitration. However, the limitation in the EU Convention to double taxation under Art 9 of the OECD Model Convention seems unduly restrictive, as other issues can and do arise.

The existence of effective arbitration procedures in tax matters is an incentive to Governments to resolve cases of international double taxation through the mutual agreement procedure. Therefore, the lack of practical case experience under the EU Convention does not mean it has failed to serve its purpose. On the contrary, the absence of arbitration proceedings reflects the resolution of double taxation through mutual agreement: a result of significant advantage to both business and Governments.

US treaty practice

For many years, the United States resisted including arbitration clauses in its double taxation Conventions. More recently, a few such clauses have been accepted. Typically, they present the following noteworthy characteristics.

- Arbitration is not compulsory. It occurs only with the consent of both competent authorities and the taxpayer.
- The arbitration is binding on all parties.
- An exception is provided so that the competent authorities will not generally accede to arbitration concerning matters of tax policy or domestic law.
- Taxpayers are provided with the right to present their views.

This approach is rather more limited than the EU Convention. While it is encouraging that such a clause has been included in certain US Conventions, the fact that arbitration is not compulsory is a major drawback. The exclusion for "tax policy or domestic law", while understandable in some respects, lacks the specificity appropriate to a provision requiring compulsory arbitration. As in the EU Convention, there are no procedural rules, which is a limitation on the effectiveness of this methodology.

Essential Facts

- The problem of "double taxation" arises where taxable profits or gains arise from sources in more than one country.
- This problem is usually remedied by specific domestic legislation and international tax treaties.
- Sources of international tax law can be found in the Statute of the International Court of Justice. The list of sources in Art 38(1) of the Statute presents a hierarchy of such sources. Of most importance are Conventions and treaties.
- Many bilateral and multilateral agreements have relevance to tax disputes, notably the OECD Model Convention on the Prevention of Double Taxation. The legal effect of these will vary depending on the constitutional make-up of the state concerned.
- Interpretation of treaties requires consideration of the attitude of the courts generally in the relevant jurisdiction and the attitude of the particular treaty in question.
- Most bilateral tax Conventions provide for arbitration procedure as a means of resolving disputes.

4 AVOIDANCE

As Lord Templeman famously stated, "... there is no morality in a tax and no illegality or immorality in a tax avoidance scheme".[1] Thus, the degree to which the issue is a problem in terms of tax law is not moral or ethical but depends very much on the definitions adopted of the particular actions in question. Conventional legal wisdom does distinguish avoidance (which is generally legal) from evasion (which is generally illegal). For the former, we have the sensible use of available reliefs and exemptions together with judicious employment of legal structures to minimise tax liability, which any taxpayer is legally entitled to do; for the latter, we have the non-declaration of income and/or assets or the making of a fraudulent return, which are evasion and subject to civil penalty and possibly criminal sanctions.

THE *RAMSAY* CASE AND ITS IMPACT

The "*Ramsay* principle" as an approach to anti-avoidance has developed from the original judgment in *IRC* v *Ramsay* delivered by the House of Lords back in 1981. Subsequent tax cases decided through the courts and beyond have interpreted, tested, stretched and even curtailed the boundaries of that original judgment.

Before *Ramsay*, the courts were reluctant to depart from a strict interpretation of tax legislation. Though not necessarily approving of tax avoidance, on a number of occasions the courts ruled in favour of the taxpayer's attempts to minimise liabilities as being generally legitimate. The courts attached importance to the principle established in *IRC* v *Duke of Westminster* (1936), in which payments were made by the taxpayer to his employees in the form of deeds of covenant, but in substance were payments of remuneration. The House of Lords refused to disregard the legal character (form) of the deeds merely because the same result (substance) could be brought about in another manner. Lord Tomlin commented:

> "Every man is entitled, if he can, to order his affairs so that the tax attaching under the appropriate Acts is less than it otherwise would be."

---

[1] *Ensign Tankers (Leasing) Ltd* v *Stokes* (1992).

This standard, coupled with high tax rates during the 1970s, encouraged complex schemes of tax avoidance, many of which were commercially artificial and carried very little financial risk. However, it transpired that the *Duke of Westminster* case was of limited application, since it contained a single tax avoidance step. The problem faced by the courts was how to deal with pre-arranged avoidance schemes containing a number of steps which clearly stretched legality and credulity.

The tax avoidance scheme under consideration in *Ramsay* was "ready-made", but the approach adopted in this and subsequent cases would have repercussions for tax planning generally.

In *Ramsay*, the company at the centre of the case sought to protect a capital gain. It therefore made two separate loans to a newly acquired subsidiary company, from funds made available by a finance house. Both loans carried interest. However, the taxpayer company subsequently reduced the interest on the first loan to nil, while interest on the second loan was doubled. The second loan was then sold to another company at a capital profit. The first loan was repaid at par and an equivalent capital loss was incurred in respect of the sale of shares in the subsidiary to another company. The taxpayer company sought relief for the capital loss, but contended that the capital profit was exempt from tax as a debt on a security. The House of Lords, whilst accepting that none of the steps involved represented a "sham", considered the scheme as a whole and held that it should be treated as a nullity for tax purposes.

In his judgment, Lord Wilberforce stated that it was not a requirement, under the *Duke of Westminster* or any other doctrine, to consider individually each separate step in a composite transaction intended to be carried through as a whole. His Lordship described the following characteristics of "circular" schemes of tax avoidance:

- First – it is a clear intention that, once started, the scheme shall proceed through the various steps to the end whether there is a contractual obligation, or merely an expectation with no practical likelihood that it will not proceed.

- Second – the taxpayer does not have to use his own funds and at the end of the scheme the taxpayer's financial position is unchanged except for the payment of fees and expenses to the scheme promoter.[2]

---

[2] The whole idea of a "promoter" now falls under legislative control, with the advent of "disclosure rules": FA 2004, ss 306–319 (as amended by FA 2008, *inter alia*); also SI 2005/1869, SI 2006/1544 and SI 2009/611 and most notably the Tax Avoidance Schemes (Information) (Amendment) Regulations 2009.

- Third – the whole and entire purpose of the scheme was the avoidance of tax.

The *Ramsay* list of tax avoidance characteristics and circumstances was modified in subsequent House of Lords decisions. In *IRC* v *Burmah Oil Co Ltd* (1982), the Lords held that the *Ramsay* principle applied to a scheme devised by the taxpayer's advisers, involving the taxpayer's own funds. Lord Diplock considered that, in order for the *Ramsay* principle to apply, there must be:

(1) a series of transactions;

(2) which are pre-ordained; and

(3) into which there are inserted steps that have no commercial purpose apart from tax avoidance.

The *Ramsay* principle had, up to this point, been confined to tax avoidance in the form of artificial schemes containing steps that were, in effect, self-cancelling. However, in *Furniss* v *Dawson* (1984), the House of Lords applied the *Ramsay* approach to a scheme of tax deferral, as opposed to avoidance, which was not circular or self-cancelling.

In *Furniss* v *Dawson*, the taxpayers wished to sell their family company shares to an independent purchaser. As part of a pre-arranged plan to defer their capital gains tax liability, the taxpayers exchanged their shares in that company for shares in a newly formed investment company (Greenjacket) incorporated in the Isle of Man. On the same day, Greenjacket sold the family company shares at the previously negotiated price. The taxpayers sought to rely on a capital gains tax exemption in respect of the company amalgamation, and a "no gain, no loss" disposal of the family company shares by Greenjacket. The High Court and Court of Appeal ruled that the *Ramsay* "principle" applied only where steps forming part of the scheme were self-cancelling. They considered that it did not allow the share exchange and sale agreements to be treated as steps in the scheme, because they had an enduring legal effect.

At the House of Lords, it was held that steps inserted in a pre-ordained series of transactions with no commercial purpose other than tax avoidance should be disregarded for tax purposes, notwithstanding that the inserted step, the introduction of Greenjacket, had a business effect. Lord Brightman stated: "that inserted step had no business purpose apart from the deferment of tax, although it had a business effect. If the sale had taken place in 1964 before capital gains tax was introduced, there would have been no Greenjacket".

The approach of the Lords to "linear" tax avoidance in *Furniss* v *Dawson* marked a significant extension of the *Ramsay* principle, which hitherto had been founded upon "circular" or self-cancelling schemes. The principle could be applied to both tax deferral and avoidance, and to situations in which the legal implications of the intermediate steps continued beyond the scheme itself. Referring to the previous criteria for the *Ramsay* principle to apply as set out in the *Burmah* case above, Lord Brightman redefined the necessary conditions:

(1) a pre-ordained series of transactions (or one single composite transaction), into which there must be

(2) steps inserted which have no commercial purpose as distinct from a business effect apart from the avoidance (or deferral) of a liability to tax.

A further development, or limitation, arose with *Craven* v *White* (1988), where the case once again proceeded to the House of Lords, who held in favour of the taxpayers, dismissing the Crown's appeal by a majority of 3 to 2. The dissenting argument was broadly that the *Ramsay* principle could be applied where the taxpayer had merely decided to carry out the scheme on an intended (taxable) transaction, if possible, by combining it with a prior avoidance transaction. However, the majority view was that a scheme was pre-ordained if it was planned as a whole and carried through as a whole, ie where the avoidance transaction was undertaken at a time when there was no "practical likelihood" that the subsequent transaction would not take place. In *Craven* v *White*, the Lords noted that there was still some uncertainty about the outcome at the start of the process. In his judgment, Lord Oliver interpreted the following requirements for *Ramsay* to apply, ie "the circumstances the court can be justified in linking the beginning with the end so as to make a single composite whole to which the fiscal results of the single composite whole are to be applied":

(1) that the series of transactions was, at the time when the intermediate transaction was entered into, pre-ordained in order to produce a given result;

(2) the intermediate transaction had no other purpose than tax mitigation;

(3) there was at the time no practical likelihood that the planned events would not take place in the order ordained, so that the intermediate transaction was not even contemplated practically as having an independent life; and

(4) that the pre-ordained events did in fact take place.

The *Ramsay* doctrine, representing a complete reversal of the rule in the *Duke of Westminster* case, in its crudest form invalidates all transactions effected solely for the purpose of avoiding liability to taxation. However, Warner J[3] clearly disagreed with the idea that the *Ramsay* principle was a legitimate, judge-made, anti-avoidance rule, which it was open to the court to mould and develop in the light of its experience in tax avoidance devices. Judges have been disinclined to apply the *Ramsay* principle but in *Furniss* Lord Brightman has confirmed the principle where the High Court and the Court of Appeal have found it a welcome release from the unfamiliar and uncomfortable obligation of determining where "the safe channel of acceptable tax avoidance shelves into the dangerous shallows of unacceptable tax evasion".[4]

In *IRC* v *McGuckian* (1997), the court considered the transfer of shares to a non-resident trustee of a settlement, followed by the rights to a dividend being assigned to a resident company for a consideration. The UK resident company then paid the amount of dividend, less a commission, to the trustee. The House of Lords considered this to be avoidance in the classic *Ramsay* mould and appeared to take a purposive approach to interpreting the law, looking at what the law is designed to achieve rather than just what it actually says.

Following this effect, however, in its decision in *MacNiven* v *Westmoreland Investments Ltd* (2001), the House of Lords reassessed the scope of the *Ramsay* principle, finding that it did not "enunciate any new legal principle"[5] that would apply to all cases but just part of "the established purposive approach to the interpretation of statutes"[6] and ruled that as the company had incurred real economic outlay in making loans to take advantage of statutory relief, this was legitimate mitigation of liability.

Most recently, in *Barclays Mercantile Business Finance Ltd* v *Mawson* (2005), Barclays bought a gas pipeline from the Irish Gas Board for £91 and leased it back to them, claiming capital allowances on the pipeline despite the negligible outlays. The Revenue cited this arrangement as "financial engineering" rather than a real purchase of plant and equipment eligible for capital allowances; however, the High Court found the arrangements perfectly acceptable as legitimate commercial activity.

---

[3] In *IRC* v *Bowater* v *Property Developments Ltd* (1985) at 798.
[4] Per Lord Scarman in *Furniss* at 156.
[5] 73 TC at 56 (para 1).
[6] 73 TC at 57 (para 6).

POST-*RAMSAY* ANTI-AVOIDANCE IN THE UK

The *Ramsay* principle, applying anti-avoidance theory to defeat circular transactions simply means that you look at the result the parties actually intended to produce and apply the ordinary fiscal consequences flowing from that result. Based on these circumstances, the Government seems to be continuing the previous practice by introducing specific legislation to combat tax avoidance and it has been argued that a properly devised GAAR[7] offers the potential for clarity for both taxpayers and tax authorities that does not exist under the *Ramsay* principle. This is because new devices for avoiding tax continue to develop. Litigation is not always the best approach for dealing with cases, because litigation in complex avoidance cases can take a long time to resolve and the uncertainty of the outcome can be prolonged considerably.[8]

Subsequently, in the last decade[9] there has been much discussion regarding the possible introduction of GAAR because the current legislation fails to work[10] effectively when the law is always one step behind sophisticated schemes. The UK has an estimated loss from tax shelters worth £13 billion per year[11] and HMRC has investigated at least one "Big Four" accounting firm in connection with a currency swap transaction.[12] Kattan[13] observed that GAAR "would act as a deterrent and stop companies from trying to get around the letter of law thereby benefiting society on the whole". This is supported by the HMRC which argues that GAAR is needed so that the tax burden is shared fairly among taxpayers. It is intended that the GAAR will apply to corporate direct taxes since companies are the main culprits in implementing aggressive tax avoidance schemes.

The UK Government declined to introduce a formal UK GAAR but has instead introduced a procedure requiring disclosure to HMRC

---

[7] General Anti-Avoidance Regulation.

[8] "A General Anti-Avoidance Rule for Direct Taxes: A Consultative Document" 4.8, p 9, available at http://www.hmrc.gov.uk/consult/consult_1.pdf as at 12 June 2006.

[9] When the Labour Government won the General Election in May 1997, it made it quite clear that it was unsatisfied with the current state of laws on to tax avoidance.

[10] O Ralph, "GAAR: Empty Threat or Deal Stopper?'" (1998) 9(9) Int Tax Review 13. Ralph compares practices and precedents across international jurisdictions, to discover the substance behind the rules.

[11] A Sparrow and G Trefgarne,"£13bn Legal Loophole to be Closed",Telegraph Online (3 March 2004), available at www.telegraph.co.uk/news/main as at 23 June 2006.

[12] I Mansell,"Revenue Widens Inquiry into Accounting Firms", *The Times*, 5 May 2004.

[13] V Kattan,"Is There A Dire Need For A General (Statutory) Anti-avoidance Rule in the UK?" available at www.pravovadurzhava.com/resources/articles/articleid/10/index.html as at 2 June 2006.

of organised schemes of tax planning.[14] The consultative documents[15] on general anti-avoidance legislation produced by the Government encouraged input from a large number of professional advisers and the industry representatives.[16] Generally, opinion suggested that the introduction of GAAR would generate a hostile environment for UK business and inward investment into the UK and would bring more uncertainty and higher costs for the taxpayer. The introduction of a GAAR is related to the key problem about methodology in interpreting and tackling tax avoidance in the UK. The experience with the general anti-avoidance systems is that the definition is normally too narrow or too broad. The HMRC definition of a transaction qualifying as tax avoidance is:

- not paying tax, paying less or paying tax later than would otherwise be the case; or
- obtaining the repayment or increased repayment, or obtaining repayment earlier than would otherwise be the case; or
- obtaining payment or increased payment by way of tax credit, or obtaining such payment earlier than would otherwise be the case.

Tax avoidance potentially alters markets and allocates resources to unproductive economic activities. Tax avoidance schemes tend to be costly for both taxpayers and tax authorities to check compliance and to resolve disputes. The suggested strategy of the former (Labour) UK Government proposed measures that would at least reduce the amount of effort wasted in avoidance of income tax, corporation tax and capital gains tax and so benefit the efficiency, effectiveness and economy in the markets through increased transparency.

What the UK is doing now is to keep under review a range of options to deter non-compliance and encourage voluntary compliance, ensuring the fairness of the tax system.[17] The aim of the disclosure rules is to limit the tax advantages that exploit loopholes and those not in line with the intention of Parliament in order to reduce tax liabilities. A unit within

---

[14] Although there is sign that the HMRC is going to launch a study on UK GAAR, available at http://www.internationaltaxreview.com/?Page=9&PUBID=210&ISS=22003&SID=638110 as at 27 June 2006.

[15] "A General Anti-Avoidance Rule for Direct Taxes: Consultative Document", via http://www. hmrc.gov.uk/consult/consult_1.pdf.

[16] The Financial Secretary to Treasury, Dawn Primolo, has urged members of the profession, business and any interested parties to come forward and express their views because the need for such legislation is questionable although it seems that the Labour Government has already made up its mind on the matter.

[17] See ss 306–319 of the Finance Act 2004, under Pt 7, titled "Disclosure of Tax Avoidance Schemes".

HMRC known as the Anti-Avoidance Group (Intelligence) conducts tax shelter analysis and assists in drafting legislation so as to close the opportunities so revealed.[18]

The user of a tax scheme is required to disclose in advance to the HMRC by entering the reference number given by the promoter[19] on their tax return and declare the commencement of that tax advantage in the year of assessment, accounting period or tax year. The major focus is on the promoter to report that he has made "the available arrangements of a broadly specified kind". In-house tax scheme from individuals, partnerships, trusts or companies must also disclose the scheme at the time the relevant tax return is due.[20] Part 2 of the Guidance described the obligation of the promoters, time limits, kind of schemes and penalties for non-compliance. The key concept of this scheme is the definition of "tax advantage", which will affect the administration of the disclosure rules. When the definition involves the avoidance of an obligation to deduct tax, it will involve a very wide range of possible ways to structure the tax scheme, such as income received in capital form or rewards designed to fall outside the provisions of the Income Tax (Earnings and Pensions) Act 2003 or the Income Tax Act 2007.

By March 2009, a total of 1,225 disclosures had been submitted and, in response, a number of provisions have been enacted; HMRC maintains that, in order to target avoidance, more needs to be done to prevent promoters from finding ways of not disclosing schemes, together with wider and more powerful disclosure regulations. In recent Finance Acts 2007–2009, it has been progressively announced that the Direct Tax Disclosure Rules would be extended and the various regulations have been rolled out, almost without pause, since.[21]

There has been a recent development in the UK with respect to the case of Marks & Spencer, whereby the ECJ reaffirmed that Member States are free to adopt law which has the specific purpose of precluding from a tax benefit wholly artificial arrangements whose purpose is to circumvent national tax law.[22] Therefore, one of the justifying arguments put forward by the Member States (which was accepted as compatible

---

[18] Inland Revenue Regulatory Impact Assessment: "Tackling Tax Avoidance" (April 2004), available at http://www.hmrc.gov.uk/ria/ as at 24 June 2006.

[19] See above at n 2.

[20] Part 1 of "Disclosure of Direct Tax Avoidance Schemes (The Main Guidance)" (July 2009).

[21] The Tax Avoidance Schemes (Prescribed Descriptions of Arrangements) Regulations 2006 (SI 2006/1543) which replaced the Tax Avoidance Schemes (Prescribed Descriptions of Arrangements) Regulations 2004 (SI 2004/1863); and see again n 2 above.

[22] (C446/03)[2006] Ch 184 (ECJ) at para 57.

with the treaty), related to tax avoidance, was the possibility that freely enabling transnational group relief would permit losses to be transferred to subsidiary companies in countries with the highest tax rates. The ECJ's stance on this case, taken with recent moves towards tax harmonisation, could be viewed as creating the conditions for a Europe-wide general anti-avoidance rule.

The ultimate question of what is acceptable and what is unacceptable tax avoidance will continue to be considered in many forums and will depend as much on attitudes in politics and society in general as it will on jurisprudence and the courts.

Essential Facts

- Tax avoidance, which is generally legal, is to be distinguished from tax evasion, which is generally illegal. Tax avoidance includes the sensible use of available reliefs and exemptions together with judicious employment of legal structures so as to minimise tax liability. Tax evasion involves the non-declaration of income and/or assets or the making of a fraudulent return, for example.
- Approaches to tax avoidance in the UK have developed from the judgment in *IRC* v *Ramsay* (1981) (see below).

Essential Cases

IRC v Duke of Westminster (1936): payments were made by the taxpayer to his employees in the form of deeds of covenant, but in substance were payments of remuneration. The House of Lords refused to disregard the form of the deeds merely because the same results could be brought about in another manner. This standard encouraged complex schemes of tax avoidance. However, it applied only to single-step schemes.

Pre-arranged schemes containing a number of steps which stretched legality and credulity were considered in **IRC v Ramsay (1981)**: a company made two separate loans to a newly acquired subsidiary company, from funds provided by a finance house. The company reduced the interest on the first loan to nil, while interest on the second loan was doubled. The second loan was then sold to another company, at a capital profit. The first loan was repaid at par and an equivalent capital loss was incurred in respect of the sale of shares in the subsidiary to another company. The taxpayer company sought relief for the capital loss, but contended that the capital profit was exempt from tax as a debt on security. The House of Lords, while accepting that none of the steps involved represented a "sham", considered the scheme as a whole and held that it should be treated as a nullity for tax purposes.

IRC v Burmah Oil Co Ltd (1982): the House of Lords held that, in order for the *Ramsay* principle to apply, there must be:

(1) a series of transactions;

(2) which are pre-ordained; and

(3) into which there are inserted steps that have no commercial purpose apart from tax avoidance.

Furniss v Dawson (1984): the House of Lords applied the *Ramsay* principle to a scheme of tax deferral, as opposed to avoidance, which was not circular or self-cancelling.

Craven v White (1988): the House of Lords held that a scheme was pre-ordained if it was planned as a whole and carried through as a whole.

Part 2

THE UK TAX SYSTEM IN PRACTICE

5 THE STRUCTURE OF THE TAX SYSTEM

"It is not the strongest of the species that survives nor the most intelligent, it is the one that is most adaptable to change."

(Charles Darwin)

THE CURRENT UK TAX MODEL

Liability to tax in the UK is, in the main, imposed by a statutory framework consisting of the annual Finance Acts which follow the budget each year; dedicated statutes which govern specific taxes within the tax regime; management statutes; and consolidation statutes which periodically bring interim developments together in a cohesive format.[1]

Examples of these latter categories are:

- *tax-specific*: the Corporation Tax Act (CTA) 2009; the Taxation of Chargeable Gains Act (TCGA) 1992; the Inheritance Tax Act (IHTA) 1984; the Value Added Tax Act (VATA) 1994; the Capital Allowances Act (CAA) 2001; the Income Tax (Earnings and Pensions) Act (ITEPA) 2003; and the Income Tax, Trading and Other Income Act (ITTOIA) 2005;
- *management*: the Taxes Management Act (TMA) 1970; and the Income Tax Act (ITA) 2007;
- *consolidation*: the Income and Corporation Taxes Act (ICTA) 1988 which is the most recent of the consolidation statutes. In many ways VATA 1983 and now VATA 1994 can also be viewed as consolidation statutes and it could also be argued that CAA 2001 and both ITEPA 2003 and ITTOIA 2005 have elements of consolidation in them. However, the main purpose certainly of the latter two statutes had more to do with modernisation and simplification of tax legislation[2] than simply consolidation of changes in the law resulting from decided cases.

All taxes, whether direct (on profits and gains) or indirect (consumption taxes), are administered by HMRC (Her Majesty's Revenue & Customs), using the powers granted under the Taxes Management Act 1970

---

[1] These statutes are collectively known as "the Taxes Acts".
[2] Under an ongoing programme of reform known as "Tax Law Rewrite", introduced under FA 1995.

mentioned above. This organisation was formed in 2004 by the merger of the former Inland Revenue, and Customs & Excise, to form a unitary tax agency.

LEGAL FRAMEWORK

Legislation

The UK tax year revolves around two main matters: the Budget delivered by the Chancellor of the Exchequer, which is usually in March,[3] and the passage of the Finance Act, which is usually introduced within 2 weeks of the Budget and, after normal parliamentary scrutiny,[4] usually passes into law the day after it receives the Royal Assent. Provisions contained in the Budget come into force on Budget Day, or if specified on another stated date such as the start of the next tax year, and are confirmed into force by passage of the Finance Act. In order to continue the financial affairs of the country between the Budget and the passage of the Finance Act, a resolution must be passed under the Provisional Collection of Taxes Act (PCTA) 1968, stating that it is "expedient in the public interest to introduce, vary or abolish a tax". This must be followed by a confirmatory resolution within 10 business days and will come into effect for the period until:

- the Finance Act becomes law;
- the PCTA resolution is rejected by Parliament;
- Parliament is dissolved.

Case law

Tax law in the UK is a statutory system structured and controlled by the process laid out above. Despite this framework there will always be areas of dispute which must be resolved by the courts. In such disputes the taxpayer may appeal in the first instance to the General Commissioners (since April 2009, to the Appeal Tribunal) or, in some specified cases, the Special Commissioners. Where the decision of the Commissioners is not acceptable, the taxpayer can appeal through the mainstream courts system

---

[3] The Budget can be at any time and there can be more than one Budget in a given year; indeed, the Budget was held in November between 1993 and 1996 to coincide with the annual spending review.

[4] Three Readings in the House of Commons; a Committee stage; Report stage; and scrutiny by the House of Lords.

of the UK, through the Court of Appeal to the new Supreme Court of the United Kingdom[5] and eventually to the European Court of Justice (ECJ). This process is set out in the Legal Framework Chart below. The objective of the courts in the UK in this instance is to ascertain the meaning of the statute, and thus to interpret the intent of Parliament in making the law. This allows for latitude in terms of statutory interpretation on the part of the judiciary, to avoid absurdity or ambiguity or to correct errors in wording. Indeed, where there is confusion or ambiguity it is now possible to refer to *Hansard* to ascertain the intentions of Parliament.[6] The role of the judiciary in interpreting statutes and thus deciding cases has at times been a contentious one, particularly in cases of alleged tax avoidance. That interesting area will be dealt with later in this work.

The Legal Process of Tax Law: TMA 1970

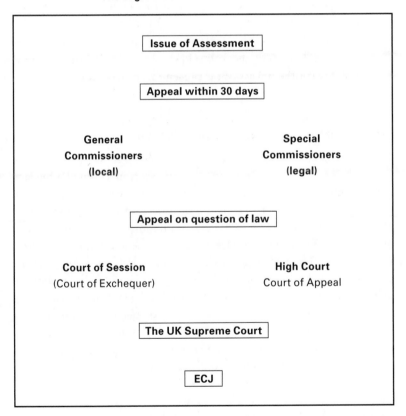

| Issue of Assessment |

| Appeal within 30 days |

| General Commissioners (local) | Special Commissioners (legal) |

| Appeal on question of law |

| Court of Session (Court of Exchequer) | High Court Court of Appeal |

| The UK Supreme Court |

| ECJ |

---

[5] Set up under the Constitutional Reform Act 2005, s 23.

[6] *Pepper* v *Hart* (1993).

European law[7]

The UK became a member of the European Economic Community (EEC), and party to its treaties, in 1973. It is now beyond argument that the UK Parliament no longer has complete power to determine the entirety of UK law. While direct taxation remains within the competence of individual Member States, of the now renamed European Union (EU), the European Court of Justice (ECJ) has made clear that Member States must exercise competence "in accordance with EC law". As a result, where a conflict arises, EC law[8] will prevail at the expense of any domestic rule. There are four incidences of impact:

- *treaties*: principal instruments of European law: primary legislation;
- *Directives*: these are incorporated into each member's domestic law: secondary legislation;
- *Regulations*: these take direct effect in Member States without domestic incorporation: secondary legislation;
- *ECJ decisions*: these are addressed to individual states and have direct impact only in those states. It is in this area in recent times that the UK has felt the impact of the pre-eminence of Europe on UK tax law.[9]

Other sources of tax law and practice

Where an anomaly is discovered in the operation of a tax statute which may result in absurdity or clear unfairness to taxpayers in abiding by the law, and the authorities do not take the view that this necessitates immediate amendment to legislation, HMRC will issue a statement, known as an Extra-Statutory Concession (ESC), indicating that it will adopt a liberal attitude to enforcement; the spirit rather than the letter of the law. Such statements are granted on a case-by-case basis and, while they can be relied upon by those in receipt of them, they are not of general application and can be withdrawn where HMRC is of the view that they are being abused. However, HMRC has been known to offer a particular taxpayer an ESC in order to avoid a certain contentious issue being tested in the courts for fear of losing the case and creating a disadvantageous precedent (to HMRC) for the generality of other taxpayers.[10]

---

[7] See Pt 1, Ch 2 of this book for more detail in this area.
[8] The law of the European Community or European Union.
[9] See *Marks & Spencer* v *Halsey* (2003).
[10] See, eg, *Mallalieu* v *Drummond* (1983).

In addition to ESCs, HMRC is from time to time given to issuing Statements of Practice, which state the interpretation that HMRC will put upon a particular area of tax law. These are by way of guidance and are designed to ensure, above all, a consistent application of the rules by all personnel in HMRC and in all parts of the UK. These do not have any legal force and cannot necessarily be relied upon by a taxpayer in court as HMRC reserves the right to invoke a different interpretation of the law where the facts of the case require and, equally, the taxpayer can argue a different interpretation or challenge the legality of such statements, during court proceedings.

DIRECT TAXES

In a simplified analysis, a taxpayer or his representative, completes a tax return and from this statement HMRC[11] produces an assessment. Tax is payable from this assessment in accordance with the system of rates and allowances which apply to the particular taxpayer in the given year of assessment, subject to the right of appeal where liability is not agreed.[12] With effect from April 1997 a system of self-assessment has been in operation which places a greater compliance burden on the taxpayer, both individual and corporate, than had been the case previously, while providing assistance to a limited degree. As outlined in Part 1 of this book, it is possible that the novelty of the Internet and some of the more esoteric judgments as to categorisations which result from this may give rise to fresh questions of tax law. Where disputes arise, these are initially dealt with at tribunal stage with a hearing before the tax commissioners,[13] wherein matters of fact and law can be considered. Commissioners' decisions can be appealed in the mainstream courts, purely on questions of law and statutory interpretation, up to the new UK Supreme Court[14] and now, beyond domestic remedy, to the European Court of Justice. As a result of this process we have a strong body of judge-made law in the UK on tax matters which is periodically subsumed into the statutory framework by means of a new consolidation statute, as mentioned above.[15]

---

[11] Her Majesty's Revenue & Customs; since 2005, the unified revenue enforcement and collection agency of the UK Treasury for all direct and indirect tax.

[12] For current rates of tax, allowances and reliefs and a detailed outline of the UK domestic tax system, see: (1) Butterworths' *Yellow Tax Handbook* (annual), and (2) Whitehouse, *Revenue Law, Principles & Practice* (18th edn).

[13] This can be either the General Commissioners or the Special Commissioners, depending on the nature of the dispute.

[14] With effect from October 2009 and replacing the House of Lords in this role and function.

[15] Currently, ICTA 1988.

In particular, in recent years, there have been several important judgments on tax avoidance which can allow the courts to intervene in commercial arrangements and disregard transactions deemed artificial where they are entered into for *avoidance* purposes.[16]

Individuals in business are classed as sole traders for income tax purposes and taxed as such if they trade in their own right. Partners in a partnership are also taxed as individuals within a rules framework which covers the tax implications of joint and several liability.[17] Additionally, all individuals must pay capital gains tax on capital profits. Where the protection of a corporate shell is chosen as the trading medium, the individuals who operate the business are classed as employees and possibly also shareholders, with the consequent implications for PAYE[18] tax and dividend taxation which result from this. The company itself will also be liable for corporation tax on both income and capital profits at a rate which varies in relation to the scale of profits resulting from its business.[19] All distributions of company assets are subject to tax whether through PAYE on the recipient or corporation tax on the company. The system of advance corporation tax (ACT), which dealt specifically with distributions such as dividends, was abolished in April 1999 in an attempt to simplify corporate taxation.[20] Issues relating to the taxation of capital gains as distinct from income and profits are considered in relation to the Internet later in this chapter.

INDIRECT TAX

VAT

Value added tax (VAT) is an indirect tax on consumers, often referred to as a turnover or transaction tax. On becoming a member of the European Community (EC), the UK replaced its existing tax on purchases with VAT,[21] as VAT must be imposed throughout the now European Union[22] on the supply of certain goods and services. As stated above, the controlling statute is now VATA 1994, as amended by the periodic Finance Acts,

---

[16] Cases which relate to what has become known as the *"Ramsay* principle"; which derive originally from *W T Ramsay* v *IRC* (1982).

[17] Traders are subject to income tax under ITTOIA 2005 (formerly Sch D to ICTA 1988).

[18] PAYE (Pay As You Earn): the standard model for the taxation of employees under Sch E to ICTA 1988. This is mandatory even where there is only one employee, who may also be a director.

[19] *Supra* 4.

[20] FA 1998, s 31.

[21] FA 1972.

[22] EC Council Directive 77/388, known in practice as the "Sixth Directive".

and the collection of the tax is the responsibility of HMRC in the UK. All persons making taxable supplies (this effectively means all businesses) whose annual turnover exceeds the given threshold, which from April 2010 is set at £68,000, must register for VAT. In respect of each trading period[23] the taxable person is obliged to complete a VAT return and pay any tax due. There are strict controls placed upon businesses as to VAT administration in relation to maintaining proper records and provision of proper customer invoices.[24] As with direct tax, there is a right of appeal against determinations of the presiding department, initially to the VAT Tribunal and thence to the mainstream courts, culminating in the European Court of Justice.

In general, VAT is charged in the UK at the standard rate, which is 17.5 per cent in the UK. However, there are three specific reliefs from the obligation to charge at this rate:

- goods or services may be subject to a lower rate, such as fuel and power or importation of antiques: all are charged at 5 per cent in the UK.
- VAT can also be levied at the zero rate, usually for social policy reasons; in the UK, for example, on most food, books and the construction of dwellings;[25]
- finally, there are exempt supplies which cover the provision of education, health and welfare and most insurance and banking services.

While the exempt supplies list is much the same throughout the EU,[26] reduced and zero-rated items vary a great deal among Member States. In practical terms the difference between an exempt supply and a zero-rated one is that a zero-rated supply is within the VAT system and thus the supplier is able to deduct input tax incurred in respect of it. VAT operates as a commercial chain from the origin or creation of goods and services through successive business stages where "value is added" and the VAT cost is offset at each stage; and ending with the consumer who pays VAT on the final product. A helpful illustration of this is given later in this book.[27]

---

[23] Normally 3-month periods but can exceptionally be 1-month or 12-month periods: VAT Regulations 1995, reg 25(1).
[24] *Supra* 16, regs 13–20.
[25] VATA 1994, Sch 8.
[26] Sixth Directive, Art 13 (as amended).
[27] Chapter 14.

In relation to e-commerce, where the use of the Internet is free then VAT issues for the provision of the service will not be relevant since VAT is not imposed where there is no consideration, ie payment, given for a supply.[28] However, where payment or other consideration, such as barter or exchange, is received for a supply made over the Internet then this will come within the VAT regime. In nearly every case where an Internet transaction is subject to VAT this will be a supply of services, unless the Internet is used merely as a mechanism for ordering goods which are to be supplied by delivery.[29]

A BUSINESS

Before commencing with any new business venture it is always important to consider what type of business structure to use. In most instances the participators will have an unrestricted choice between corporate and non-corporate trading. The only legal restriction is that, with the exception of certain professions such as solicitors and accountants, partnerships are limited to a maximum of 20 partners.[30] In terms of tax considerations the choices may be more complex than it would appear at first glance. For a small but successful business, despite the attractions of limited liability, a limited company is not necessarily the best idea; sometimes a partnership provides the better solution. If you compare the effective tax rates payable in the two models, the company and its shareholders (which in the case of a new, small-scale venture may be largely the same persons) between them can pay tax on distributed income at a rate of around 50 per cent, whereas partners in a partnership pay tax at a maximum of 40 per cent. In contrast, the true value of the company model is not the obvious one of corporate limited liability, but that where the profits are retained within the business the effective tax rate is 19 per cent for small companies and a maximum of 30 per cent for companies with profits over £1.5 million.[31] This may be an attractive option in a scenario where rapid growth is top of the business agenda. However, it should be noted that it is relatively easy to incorporate an established business from a sole trading concern or partnership[32] but more complex to do this in reverse.[33]

---

[28] VATA 1994, s 5(2)(a).
[29] Note the anomalous situation of digital products which is dealt with in Pt 1, Ch 2.
[30] Companies Act 1985, s 716 and Companies Act 2006, Pt 2.
[31] The first £10,000 of company profits are free of tax, and marginal relief applies between the small and mainstream companies rates.
[32] Capital gains roll over relief: TCGA 1992, s 162.
[33] See Whitehouse, *Revenue Law, Principles & Practice* (27th edn, 2009), Ch 46.

The typical partnership will involve a number of partners with unlimited personal liability and the typical company will be a private limited company not open to public subscription of its shares. Other possibilities exist as variations on the typical options, such as:

- *the plc (public limited company)*: this has attractions for an established business and allows for raising funds from the public, which is not open to private companies.[34] Not an option for a business starting from scratch;

- *the unlimited company*: this option has few corporate advantages other than a greater degree of secrecy, and places shareholders in the same position as partners;

- *the limited partnership*: this can only apply in strictly controlled circumstances, as a means of bringing in investment, and cannot apply to all participators. The controlling partners must still expose themselves to unlimited liability;

- *company/partnerships*: a complex option involving a hybrid arrangement where individuals join in partnership with a limited company, which is a distinct legal person. This can allow flexibility in the allocation of profits between the corporate and non-corporate entity, to maximise tax advantage;

- *LLP (limited liability partnership)*: a partnership/corporate hybrid which arose as a solution to problems of traditional partnerships incurring liability for client advice in large transactions. None of the members are exposed for the debts of the firm.[35]

Deductions and capital allowances

A major concern to all businesses is the overall efficiency of the business model chosen. Rather than just in terms of a simple comparison of tax rates, more subtle considerations often apply depending on the detailed nature of the trade and the business plan envisaged by the participators. Decisions as to business structure will involve consideration of a range of taxation and non-taxation factors.

Revenue expenditure

One key element of concern to businesses is whether items of expenditure are deductible in computing the taxable profits. Income profits for a trading

---

[34] Companies Act 1985, s 81 and Companies Act 2006, Pts 1–6.
[35] Limited Liability Partnerships Act 2001.

concern are computed under the rules of ITTOIA 2005,[36] whether the business is incorporated or not as in this sense corporation tax is merely an aspect of income tax. Similarly, the rules for allowable deductions by individuals and partnerships apply equally to companies. Under ICTA 1988, s 74, it is clearly stated in relation to the computation of taxable profits that:

> "no sum shall be deducted in respect of –
>
> (a) any disbursements or expenses, not being money wholly and exclusively laid out or expended for the purposes of the trade, profession or vocation".

Clearly, expenditure incurred in setting up any business, or as it may be in this case, in establishing an Internet presence, will satisfy the above statutory test.[37] This will be the case even if the material provided via the Internet is in itself free, since the underlying business plan may be to achieve profits indirectly from advertising revenue which results from customer "hits" on the site.

Capital expenditure

Capital expenses are not deductible from trading profits; however, a system of capital allowances permits the writing-off of capital expenditure over the lifetime of the asset involved. Principally, this relates to "plant and machinery", and although neither term has been defined in statute, case law assists where there is doubt as to categorisation, which more commonly occurs in relation to "plant" than "machinery".[38] Generally, machinery is regarded as assets with moving parts such as engines, pumps or lifts, whereas plant is commonly held to be assets which are used in the course of a trade but which cannot be regarded simply as premises.[39] There is a separate system of allowances which deal with premises such as offices, factories etc.[40] For an Internet business, computers and other electronic apparatus will qualify as "plant" for capital allowances. Even although computers are "machines", it is accepted that electronic apparatus, including wiring and peripherals, can be regarded as "plant".[41]

---

[36] Formerly Sch D, Case 1.
[37] For guidance on the strictness of the statutory test under ICTA 1988, s 74, see *Bentleys, Stokes & Lewless v Beeson* (1952).
[38] See *Yarmouth v France* (1887).
[39] See *Gray v Seymours Garden Centre* (1995).
[40] CAA 1990, ss 1–21.
[41] See *Cole Bros Ltd v Phillips* (1982).

Computer software qualifies for capital allowances as a result of specific amendment to the legislation,[42] though the option still remains to regard software as a revenue cost if, for example, it is transitory or requires regular update and renewal. "Software" in this context includes all types of package, whether off-the-shelf, or bundled with hardware, and capital allowances are also available to offset the cost of developing in-house or bespoke software.

The Finance Act 2000[43] contains extended provisions on capital allowances, for the promotion of e-commerce in the UK. These provisions are aimed at small and medium-sized businesses and are designed to allow a cashflow benefit on new investment to encourage growth. Specifically the measures are twofold:

- small businesses can now claim 100 per cent FYAs (first year allowances) on their investments in "information and communication technology" from tax year 2000–01, for 3 years. They can therefore write off the full cost of such investments against taxable income;
- small and medium-sized businesses can continue to claim 40 per cent FYAs on all machinery and plant. This is an indefinite extension to the relief introduced temporarily under previous legislation.[44]

The legislation uses the same criteria as the Companies Act 1989 to define a "small" and a "medium-sized" business, but applies the relief to incorporated and non-incorporated concerns.

	Small	*Medium-sized*
Turnover: not more than:	£5.6m	£22.8m
Assets: not more than:	£2.8m	£11.4m
Employees: not more than:	50	250

CAPITAL GAINS TAX

Capital gains tax is charged on any gain resulting when a chargeable person makes a chargeable disposal of a chargeable asset. Tax is charged on the amount of gain left after taking into account any exemptions or reliefs and after deducting any allowable losses.[45]

---

[42] CAA 1990, s 67A, as introduced by FA (No 2) 1992.
[43] See FA 2000, ss 69, 70 and 71.
[44] F(No2)A, 1997, FA 1998 and FA 1999.
[45] TCGA 1992, ss 2–21.

In April 1998 the UK Government introduced capital gains tax taper relief to create incentives for investment in assets generating growth. The tax rates are lowered by reducing the amount of gain brought into charge, the longer the asset has been held. From April 2000 the taper leads to an effective rate of 10 per cent on a business asset held for at least 4 years. Business assets include, in this context, shareholdings in a trading company. This relief is of particular help to a new business attempting to grow in a relatively short time period, which then might float or sell on to a larger concern; a pattern noticeable in e-business.

Another area of particular importance, especially in the virtual world of e-commerce, which potentially gives rise to capital gains exposure is Intellectual Property (IP). As stated above, capital gains legislation applies on the *acquisition and disposal of assets* whether tangible or intangible, and IP rights include:

- *trade marks*: these include domain names in e-commerce (amazon. co.uk; inlandrevenue.gov.uk etc), also slogans, sounds and business logos;
- *inventions and designs*: new technological innovations, eg website styles, should be patented before going public;
- *copyright*: dated records should be retained to ensure that proof of ownership is available.

Ensuring proper protection for IP rights will guarantee the right to disposal proceeds for such assets without challenge provided the right concerned can be represented in some graphical form, or by means of a colour, smell or sound.[46] From a tax perspective, business reliefs available to set against capital gains liability where, for example, the gains are re-invested in an existing or new business venture, make this strategy beneficial as well as legally sensible for the protection of rights.[47]

SPECIAL INVESTMENT SCHEMES

The main investment schemes currently available to encourage investment in new ventures are: the Enterprise Investment Scheme (EIS) and Venture Capital Trusts (VCTs). Both provide a range of tax-based incentives for individuals to invest in small, higher-risk unquoted trading companies. EIS facilitates direct investment in the companies while VCTs caters for

[46] Trade Marks Act 1994.
[47] TCGA 1992, ss 152–159, 162 and 164.

indirect investment through a quoted investment fund. Both give 20 per cent income tax relief on the investment, coupled with exemption from capital gains tax on any gain, provided the investment is held for 5 years.[48]

Added to these, more recently introduced incentives under the Enterprise Management Incentive allow up to 15 key employees to receive share options up to £100,000. The options will attract no income tax nor national insurance charge and will pay capital gains tax on realisation subject to taper relief down to a tax rate of 10 per cent after 4 years' holding.[49] Further general profit share, and share ownership, plans apply to all employees and allow a range of tax incentives for participating businesses and their employees,[50] ranging from exemption from tax and national insurance to limitation of capital gains.

PERSONAL LIABILITY TO TAX

An individual taxpayer's liability is calculated by aggregating that individual's income from all sources while listing each category of income separately. The income is divided by category, as follows:

- non-savings income, including earnings from employment, profits from trades and professions and income from property;
- savings income (excluding dividends from UK companies), including interest and other annual payments such as purchased life annuities;
- dividends from UK companies: these carry a one-ninth tax credit and are always listed gross in the computation.

In most instances tax is assessed on income actually received during a particular year of assessment (tax year); thus, only amounts actually paid to the taxpayer in the period 6 April 2010 to 5 April 2011 are chargeable to tax in the tax year 2010–11. An exception to this exists in relation to business profits which are related to the accounting period of the business in question and assessed on a current-year basis, thus, the accounting period of the relevant business which ends during the current year of assessment. Profits from a trade which has its accounting period to 30 June 2010 will be taxed in the year of assessment 2010–11. Special arrangements are made

---

[48] TCGA 1992, ss 150 and 151.
[49] FA 2000, s 61 and Sch 14.
[50] FA 2000, ss 47 and 49 and Sch 8.

under the Taxes Acts for the commencement and closure of a trading business and also for changes of accounting date.[51]

Appeals

Right of appeal: the taxpayer generally has a right of appeal against any formal decision by an inspector or the Board of HM Revenue & Customs, the majority of appeals made being against assessments.

Time limits: appeals must normally be made within 30 days after the date of the issue of the assessment (or the amendment to the self-assessment) although HM Revenue & Customs may accept a late appeal where there is a reasonable excuse for the delay. The appeal must state the grounds on which the appeal is being made (eg that HM Revenue & Customs' amendment is incorrect).

Procedures: where an appeal is not settled between a taxpayer and an inspector, it is listed for hearing by the Appeal Tribunal (since April 2009; formerly the Tax Commissioners).

First-tier Tribunal: most appeals are heard in private by the First tier, including most appeals concerning personal allowances and other reliefs.

Second-tier Tribunal: certain specialist appeals are heard by the Special Commissioners, including decisions regarding deduction of tax at source, appeals against assessments made by the Board and a number of technical matters, mainly overseas matters or regarding financial bodies. The appeals heard by the Special Commissioners are generally in public and selected decisions are reported.

Courts: decisions of the Commissioners on matters of fact are normally binding on both parties. If either party is dissatisfied, an appeal on a point of *law* may then be made to the High Court, then to the Court of Appeal and, finally, if leave is granted, to the UK Supreme Court.

---

[51] ICTA 1988, ss 198, 199–202 and 312–314; and ITA 2007.

Essential Facts

- Liability to tax in the UK is largely imposed by a statutory framework of annual Finance Acts, dedicated tax statutes, management statutes and consolidation statutes.

- All UK taxes are administered by HMRC, formed by the merger of the former Inland Revenue and Customs & Excise.

- The Budget, usually delivered in March each year, and the subsequent Finance Act are the main elements in the UK tax year.

- Although tax law in the UK is a statutory system, case law has developed from interpretation of decisions of the General Commissioners, the Special Commissioners, the Court of Appeal, the House of Lords and the European Court of Justice.

- Since the UK became a member of the EEC, now the EU, the ECJ has made it clear that Member States must exercise competence "in accordance with EC law".

- Extra Statutory Concessions and Statements of Practice are issued by HMRC by way of guidance on the operation of tax laws.

- For direct taxes, a taxpayer completes a tax return from which HMRC produces an assessment. Indirect taxes are levied on the supply of goods or services.

- A new business venture will have a choice of the type of business structure to be used: public limited company, private limited company, unlimited company, limited partnership, company partnership or sole trader.

- The tax efficiency of the business model is important.

- Capital gains tax is charged on any gain resulting when a chargeable person makes a chargeable disposal of a chargeable asset.

- The main investment schemes available to encourage investment in new ventures are: the Enterprise Investment Scheme (EIS) and Venture Capital Trusts (VCTs).

- An individual's tax liability is calculated by aggregating that individual's income from all sources while listing each category of income separately.

- The taxpayer generally has a right of appeal against any formal decision by an inspector of HMRC to the General or Special Commissioners or, on appeal, to the courts.

Essential Cases

Pepper v Hart (1993): where there is confusion or ambiguity in the interpretation of a statute, it is possible to refer to *Hansard* to ascertain the intentions of Parliament.

6 PERSONAL INCOME TAXATION

In the UK, the concept of income is based on three straightforward criteria:

(1) that the sum involved should fall within one of the statutory heads of charge;

(2) that it should be of a revenue nature and not capital;[1]

(3) that it should not be specifically exempted by statute.[2]

Income tax is generally paid by individual legal persons at certain rates[3] which means that entities other than individual living persons are liable for income tax or variations thereof. Trusts, estates in the course of administration, partnerships,[4] and corporate entities of various types are all liable for income tax in some form.[5] Income tax is paid currently at a starting rate, a basic rate and a higher rate and is applied differentially between several categories and types of income, with special treatment for savings and dividend income.[6] The old UK schedular system of income tax listed six Schedules (A–F) but two have been repealed (B and C) and the remaining four have been rewritten by ITEPA 2003 and ITTOIA 2005. It is clear that these new legislative measures have done more reorganising than radical alteration of the tax law of the UK and thus all the case law which is relevant to an understanding of the law is based on the old system. This will only change over time as new cases are decided. The major consolidation statute for tax law remains the Income and Corporation Taxes Act 1988 and the territorial scope of UK income tax remains unchanged in that residents are charged on their worldwide income and non-residents on their income arising in the UK.

---

[1] *Moss Empires Ltd* v *IRC* (1937); generally profits are income only if they possess a quality of recurrence.

[2] This last category has been much clarified and simplified by recent legislation under "Tax Law Rewrite", ITEPA 2003 and ITTOIA 2005.

[3] ICTA 1988, s 1.

[4] This has recently been altered so that in fact each partner has individual personal liability as well as joint and several liability.

[5] UK companies pay corporation tax but this is income tax for companies and interacts with the income tax system through the various potential sources of company income; foreign companies can still pay income tax.

[6] See the rates and allowances tables in the Appendix.

THE NEW ARRANGEMENTS

ICTA 1988, s 1(1), as amended by ITEPA 2003 and ITTOIA 2005, lists eight heads of charge for income:

(1) amounts charged under ITEPA 2003, Pt 2 – employment income. This charge also covers matters which arise under Pts 3–5 – earnings, deductions and exemptions;

(2) amounts charged under ITEPA 2003, Pt 9 – pension income;

(3) amounts charged under ITEPA 2003, Pt 10 – social security income;

(4) amounts charged under ITTOIA 2005, Pt 2 – trading income, which covers all trades and professions;

(5) amounts charged under ITTOIA 2005, Pt 3 – property income (land, rent and premiums);

(6) amounts charged under ITTOIA 2005, Pt 4 – savings and investment income;

(7) amounts charged under ITTOIA 2005, Pt 5 – miscellaneous income;

(8) any other amounts which, under the Taxes Acts, are charged to income tax.

THE SCHEDULES

The old system of Schedules was in its most recent form set out as follows, with Schs A, D, E and F covering the arrangements for charges to income tax set out in the new arrangements above as follows:

- Sch A (ICTA 1988, s 15): still applies largely for corporation tax but for income tax is now in ITTOIA 2005, Pt 3;
- Sch D (ICTA 1988, s 18): still applies for corporation tax, and is subdivided into six "Cases":
  - Case I: profits or gains from a trade, now in ITTOIA 2005, Pt 2;
  - Case II: profits or gains from a profession or vocation, now in ITTOIA 2005, Pt 2;
  - Case III: interest, annuities and other annual payments, now in ITTOIA 2005, Pts 4 and 5;
  - Case V: income from foreign possessions, now in ITTOIA 2005, Pt 4;

- Case VI: annual profits or gains "not falling under any other Case or Schedule", now in ITTOIA 2005, Pt 5;
- Sch E (ICTA 1988, s 19): taxed emoluments from an office or employment and was almost entirely covered by the PAYE system of collection,[7] now in ITEPA 2003, Pt 2;
- Sch F (ICTA 1988, s 20): taxed distributions by companies resident in the UK, now in ITTOIA 2005, Pt 4.

SELF-ASSESSMENT

The system of self-assessment of tax for individuals was introduced in the UK in the tax year 1996–97[8] and fundamentally altered the balance of the legal obligation between the taxpayer and the tax authority by transferring the responsibility for calculating and settling tax liabilities to the taxpayer. HMRC can require any taxpayer to complete and submit a tax return; however, the majority, who have straightforward arrangements which involve their income being taxed at source and who are not higher rate taxpayers, are not normally required to do so. The legal onus as to whether a return should or should not be completed in given circumstances ultimately lies with the taxpayer, so, where there is a change of circumstances which may result in a new or increased level of income, HMRC should be notified and a return sought. A tax return is usually a standard 10-page document (SA100) which has, in addition, supplementary pages to cover other specific events or types of income (such as a second employment, partnerships, rental income, capital gains etc) and these extra pages can been obtained from HMRC on request. HMRC is able to accept returns in an electronic format as well as a physical document and these can be submitted live online using Internet technology.[9]

Disclosure rules relating to the prevention of tax avoidance have added an additional compliance burden to the legal obligations under self-assessment, both on the taxpayer himself and also on any professional adviser he may engage to assist in the structuring of his tax affairs and preparation of business accounts and tax returns.[10]

---

[7] PAYE: Pay As You Earn – direct collection by employers of tax and national insurance due by their employees under a statutory obligation.

[8] FA 1995; FA 1996; and TMA 1970, ss 8 and 8A.

[9] TMA 1970, Sch 3A and FA 1999, s 132.

[10] FA 2004, ss 306–319, brought into effect from 1 August 2004 and subsequently enhanced by FA 2005–2009.

Filing the return – relevant dates

The tax return (Form SA 100) is usually issued by HM Revenue & Customs during April, shortly after the end of the tax year.

Filing date – The return must normally be completed and submitted by	*31 January* following the tax year to which it relates.
Where a return is not issued until after 31 October following the tax year, the filing date is extended to	3 months from the date the return is issued.
If a taxpayer wishes the HMRC to calculate his tax, the return must be submitted by	*30 September* following the tax year (or within 2 months after the return is received, if later).
Where employees wish to have a tax underpayment of up to £2,000 collected in a later year through the PAYE scheme, the return must be submitted by	*30 September* following the tax year (or within 2 months after the return is received, if later).

Corrections and amendments – relevant dates

HM Revenue & Customs has 9 months from receiving the return in which to correct obvious errors. The correction does not take effect if the taxpayer gives notice to HM Revenue & Customs, rejecting it within 30 days.

A taxpayer may also make amendments to the return, by notifying HM Revenue & Customs within a year from the filing date. However, a penalty may still be imposed if there is evidence that the original return was made fraudulently or negligently.

If a taxpayer fails to submit a return or fails to notify a liability to tax, even where a return has not been required, there are a variety of legal consequences under the Taxes Management Act 1970. As well as penalties for late filing or failing to notify, the HMRC will issue a determination of the amount of tax due which is estimated in accordance with the information available to it[11] and this estimate will become the substantive tax bill until or unless the taxpayer replaces it with agreed accurate figures or successfully appeals the estimate through the commissioners and the

---

[11] TMA 1970, s 28.

courts.[12] A taxpayer is normally required to complete and file a tax return, where one has been issued, or notify a new source of taxable income, by 31 January following the end of a given tax year; thus by 31 January 2007 for the tax year which ran from April 2005 until April 2006 (see "relevant dates" above). Income tax, not covered under the PAYE scheme, is normally required to be paid in two instalments on the 31 January, the deadline date for returns, and 31 July following. Where there has been a dispute as to liability, an appeal, an investigation or a delay in otherwise issuing a liability notice by HMRC, then the due date for payment is 3 months after the issue of an agreed liability notice.[13]

INCOME TAX COMPUTATION

An individual taxpayer's income from all sources must be aggregated together to make a computation of liability, while keeping each category of income separate. The categories used to make up the computation are as follows:

- non-savings income: includes all earned income and also property income:
- savings income: other than dividends from UK companies. For computation purposes, all income must be entered "gross" without deduction of tax at source, and thus pre-taxed income must be "grossed up" at the correct rate of tax as deducted, typically 22 per cent. Savings income includes interest from banks and building societies, purchased life annuities, foreign income taxable under Sch D, Cases IV and V;
- dividends from UK companies; these must be grossed up at 100/90 to take account of deduction at source.

The basis of assessment is current year, which for most types of income means that it is liable to tax at the time of receipt; however, for trading and professional income the profits assessed in a tax year are those of the accounting period which ended during that tax year. Thus, while PAYE liability in the tax year 2010–11 relates to the tax charged on a monthly or weekly basis on earnings as they are received throughout the tax year, profits for a trading year ending 30 May 2010 or 31 October 2010, would

---

[12] See Appeals in Pt 1 of this work at p 64.
[13] TMA 1970, ss 55 and 59.

be taxed in 2010–11 even though much of the trade occurred in another tax year.[14]

Deductions, allowances and reliefs

Certain permitted statutory deductions, allowances and reliefs are permitted to be set against the taxpayer's aggregated total income prior to applying income tax.

Charges on income are the first of these, usually compulsory payments of interest on approved loans or a co-operative investment, which are deductible from any of the three categories of income.[15] Payments to charities under the Gift Aid scheme are the next, and relief is given by an extension to the basic rate band of tax; thus tax relief at 20 per cent is refunded to the recipient on payment of the gift, subject to proof using a standard signed form. At this stage the aggregated total income after such deductions is known as the statutory total income (STI).

Personal allowances come next, with three types deducted from the STI to arrive at the individual taxpayer's taxable income (TI), subject to certain special investment reliefs which may apply from time to time.[16] The three categories are: the individual personal allowance (ICTA 1988, s 257(1)); the age allowance (ICTA 1988, s 257(2)), and the blind person's allowance (ICTA 1988, s 265). There is also a residual additional age-related allowance for married couples which applies where at least one of the parties was born prior to 6 April 1935. This relates to the former rules which gave increased tax allowances to all married couples; and, with the exception of elderly people, it has been gradually phased out since the introduction of self-assessment.

NATIONAL INSURANCE IN PERSONAL TAX

Where an employee receives earnings, national insurance contributions (NICs) have to be accounted for as a contributions cost to both the employer and the employee. Often seen as a hidden tax on employment and as additional income tax by stealth, NICs are officially the funding mechanism for the state pension and the provider of core funding for the NHS, despite the fact that the monies raised from NICs is not hypothecated specifically for these purposes. NICs are categorised into

---

[14] ICTA 1988, s 198.
[15] ICTA 1988, ss 359–362.
[16] Special investment reliefs currently available are EIS (Enterprise Investment Scheme: ICTA 1988, Sch 15B) and VCT (Venture Capital Trusts: ICTA 1988, s 289A).

Tax computation with reliefs and deductions – example

Max trades in a retail outlet, drawing up accounts to 30 June. In the year ended 30 June 2005 he makes a loss of £5,468. He is also a partner in a separate trade and, for 2009–10, his share of the assessable profit is £33,775. He claims to set off his trading loss against his other income for 2009–10. His other income and payments for 2009–10 are as follows:

	£
Building society interest (net)	3,200
Dividends from UK companies (net)	6,750

	£	£
Trading profit		33,775
Interest (2,000 + 1,200)	3,200	
Add: tax deducted @ 20% (£3,200 x 1/4)	800	
		4,000
UK dividends	6,750	
Add: tax credit (£6,750 x 1/9)	750	
		7,500
Total income		£45,275
Loss relief (under TA 1988, s 380)	5,468	
Total deductions		5,468
Total income less deductions		39,807
Personal allowance		6,475
Taxable income		33,332

Tax payable:		
Non-savings income:	2,440 @ 10%	244.00
	19,392 @ 20%	3,878.40
Interest income	4,000 @ 20%	800.00
Dividend income:		
Balance remaining in basic rate band	7,500 @ 10%	750.00
		5,672.40
Tax credits and tax deducted at source		1,550.00
		£4,122.40

Classes: Classes 2 and 4 relate to profits from self-employment and are paid as a percentage of profits within certain thresholds; Class 3 is an additional voluntary contribution to cover periods of absence abroad, preventing a shortfall in overall lifetime contributions for pension purposes. Classes 1, 1A and 1B relate to employment income with both employers and employees paying Class 1, and Classes 1A and 1B being employer-only contributions. Class 1 NICs are deducted from salary and paid to the Government under the PAYE scheme, subject to a series of thresholds and ceilings depending on status and earnings (see chart above). The additional employers' contributions add a significant burden to employers' costs in employing staff as they are paid as a percentage of salary additional to the salary figure, and many tax avoidance schemes in the employment field have the aim of reducing the employers' NIC costs. This obligation on employers has led in the past to the provision of benefits in kind to employees in the form of goods and services, which were outwith the PAYE/NIC system and thus reduced the overall cost to the employer of employing staff while giving staff goods and services at cost price as a perk[17] of a particular employment tax free instead of additional, taxable pay. To prevent such arrangements, frequent legislation has been introduced over time to bring all such benefits (cars, accommodation, holiday vouchers, mobile phones, subsidised meals etc) within the scope of the PAYE system. As this process has continued, more taxpayers have sought to place themselves within the more beneficial self-employed regime for tax and particularly NICs, and this process has been resisted by the tax authorities for obvious reasons of loss of revenue. In Budget Press Release IR35, on 9 March 1999, the Chancellor of the Exchequer announced changes to anti-avoidance measures in the area of personal service provision.[18] The measure, disguised as an anti-avoidance provision, had serious consequences for those involved in the provision of services through personal service companies. As Burton J put it: "the reality is that if the service company is indeed substantially or wholly captured by IR35, then it will pay more tax".[19]

IR35's stated intention was to prevent employees setting up a company and performing their usual job through a personal service company intermediary in order to gain the resulting tax advantages. However, the wide drafting of the measure resulted in many legitimate contract

---

[17] "Perk": a perquisite of employment.

[18] Budget 1999: Press Notices, IR35. "Countering Avoidance in the Provision of Personal Services" from Treasury website www.hm-treasury.gov.uk (accessed 24 November 2005).

[19] *R (on the application of Professional Contractors Group Ltd and Others) v IRC* (2001).

workers being deemed as "disguised employees". The Government was keen to ensure that service companies and partnerships engaged through intermediaries could not take advantage of reduced tax and national insurance if they were "disguised employees". However, this controversy and the sledgehammer approach to those whose working arrangements left them vulnerable to the imposition of extra tax, has led to a more considered view[20] aimed at creating an equity-based treatment of workers who perform the same economic function.

BUSINESS TAXATION

So far in this chapter we have outlined the situation as it might apply to an individual in general or typical terms where there might be employment or mixed income situations. We will now examine the situation from the perspective of those engaging in a trade or profession: self-employment. As shown above, ITTOIA 2005, Pt 2 now deals with all "trading income" which includes "trades, professions and vocations" as they were previously known under Cases I and II of Sch D under the old scheduler system. What has not changed with the new regime are the problems around defining what constitutes "trading" (and is therefore subject to income tax) and what is not (and is therefore exempt, but possibly subject to capital taxation). The legislation has kept its definition of "trade" very loose, to allow flexibility to the courts, and states that trade "includes every trade, manufacture, adventure or concern in the nature of trade".[21] Thus, we use case authority and other jurisprudence for guidance as to what is and is not involved. The Royal Commission on the Taxation of Profits and Income[22] produced an approach which pulled together the decided cases on the pertinent issues up to that time and this has become normal practice. The approach involves a series of tests to be applied to the activity in question which, taken together, would indicate whether trading was taking place or not. These six tests, with a seventh imputed at a later stage, are known as the "badges of trade" and, while none is in and of itself conclusive, they are the yardsticks for professional and trade bodies, HMRC and the courts. They are as follows:

(1) *subject-matter of the transaction*: if the property at the core of the activity does not provide personal enjoyment to its owner but is a

---

[20] See Professor Judith Freeman's report for the Tax Law Review Committee of the IFS (2001).
[21] ICTA 1988, s 832.
[22] (1955) Cmd 9474.

typical commodity normally used in trade, the transaction will be considered to be trading;[23]

(2) *frequency of similar transactions*: a single transaction can be considered to be trading, however repeated transactions in the same methodology is a clear indication of trade;[24]

(3) *circumstances responsible for the realisation*: a forced sale to raise cash creates a presumption against trade, as does the disposal of assets by receivers in a company, or executors in an estate;[25]

(4) *supplementary work on the property realised*: work done on the property to make it more marketable or when steps are taken to organise the business with a view to sales is good evidence of trading;[26]

(5) *motive for the transaction*: where a transaction is undertaken with the intention of making a profit, this is evidence of trading – however, the absence of a clear profit motive does not preclude the conclusion that trade has taken place;[27]

(6) *length of ownership*: a quick sale is more suggestive of trading and a long period of ownership more suggestive of an investment, though these are not absolutes.[28]

The putative seventh badge which has been suggested subsequently is that of "specialist skill", which might add weight to circumstantial evidence of trade.

Income tax is charged on the full amount of the trading profits, after allowable deductions and reliefs, under ITTOIA 2005, s 7, based on the business accounts which are to be prepared in accordance with generally accepted accounting practice.[29] Expenditure cannot be deducted in computing the profits of a business if it is prohibited by the Taxes Acts[30] or ITTOIA 2005.

- Capital expenditure is not deductible in computing profits.[31]

23 *Rutledge v IRC* (1929); *IRC v Reinhold* (1953); *Marson v Morton* (1986).
24 *Pickford v Quirke* (1927); *Leach v Pogson* (1962).
25 *Stott v Hoddinott* (1916); *IRC v The Old Bushmills Distillery Co Ltd* (1927).
26 *Taylor v Good* (1974); *Cape Brandy Syndicate v IRC* (1921); *Martin v Lowry* (1927).
27 *Ensign Tankers (Leasing) Ltd v Stokes* (1992); *Wisdom v Chamberlain* (1969).
28 *Turner v Last* (1965); *Eames v Stepnell Properties Ltd* (1967).
29 For a full discussion of the accounting aspects of business accounts for tax purposes, see *Revenue Law Principles and Practice* (24th edn), Ch 10.
30 ICTA 1988, s 9.
31 *Lawson v Johnson Matthey* (1992).

- The deduction must be incurred *wholly and exclusively* for the purposes of the trade.[32]

Traders must keep an ongoing valuation of their trading stock (or work in progress in the case of professions where the stock in trade is of an intangible nature) and this must be listed in accounts at the end of each trading period and thus reflected in the taxable profits. This reflects matters like work as yet unbilled or stock which has not yet been sold and thus should not be taxed as income but allowed as a deduction and also reflects assets held within a business capable of future profit realisation.

Example: Willcotrade

A market trader with a very simple business structure and few overheads measures his business as follows:

	£	£
Product sales in year		62,000
Opening stock	18,300	
Stock purchased in year	29,000	
Less Closing stock	(24,100)	
Cost of sales		23,200
Profit		38,800

A trader is not obliged to make a profit on each transaction or sale in the course of business but must make an account of the actual sum received. However, there are certain exceptions to this:

- *transfer pricing situations*:[33] where there are businesses trading across jurisdictional borders these rules prevent the movement of goods and services at "less than arm's length" prices to obtain a tax advantage;
- the rule in *Sharkey* v *Wernher* (1956): where there is a disposal of an item of trade stock or business goods otherwise than in the ordinary course of business, it must be brought into account at its market value at the date of the transaction. In the case in question, the taxpayer ran a stud farm, commercial breeding horses, and also raced horses for pleasure. When she transferred five horses from the stud farm

---

[32] ITTOIA 2005, s 34; ICTA 1988, s 74; and see *Caillebotte* v *Quinn* (1975), *Mallalieu* v *Drummond* (1983) and *McKnight* v *Sheppard* (1997).
[33] ICTA 1988, s 770A and Sch 28AA.

to the racing stable, the Revenue disputed the transaction and the House of Lords found that the market value of the horses must be accounted for, not the cost price.

This "market value" rule is subject to two caveats: first, it is only relevant when the disposal or use of stock is not a genuine trading transaction or part of a trade promotion justifiable on commercial grounds; and, second, the rule does not apply to professional persons[34] such as authors.

Example: Technomusic

This business sells computers and electrical equipment from a website. As a sales promotion, the owners offer a free MP3 player (worth £100) to customers buying any full computer or sound system, these typically costing £600–£800. *Sharkey* v *Wernher* does not apply as this is a commercial disposition to promote the business and the cost can be written off from stock.

The method of valuation of stock or work in progress is not stipulated in statute, but good accounting practice must be followed in such situations in a consistent manner. However, where a discontinuance of trade is involved, the principle established in *IRC* v *Cock Russell & Co Ltd* (1949) must be applied, which states that stock etc must be valued at the lower of its cost price and the market value, where the market value is that typically available in the particular business or trade.[35]

Basis of assessment

Individuals or those in partnership together can commence or cease business at any time and can therefore choose an accounting date on these terms and these dates need not coincide with the tax year. This may lead to difficulties in matching up periods of trade with years of assessment and in particular it may cause problems on commencement and cessation of trade. Tax is assessed and calculated on a current-year basis[36] and there are special measures to deal with the opening and closing years and for any changes of accounting date during the trading life of the business. The effect of taxing profits on trading periods and matching them to tax years means that some profits will be taxable more than once because the profits of an accounting (or trading) period overlap two tax years. However, there are rules for overlapping profits to ensure that the business is taxed over

---

[34] *Mason* v *Innes* (1967).
[35] *BSC Footwear* v *Ridgeway* (1972); but see also ITTOIA 2005, ss 173–181.
[36] ITTOIA 2005, ss 197–220.

its life on the actual profits made, by providing overlap relief.[37] The relief may be claimed when the business ceases or is sold or where there is a long basis period as a result of a change of accounting date.

Example: opening and closing years

ACME Trading

ACME starts trading on 1 July 2004 and has a standard year with accounts to 30 June 2005

The profits are shown as:

	£
Year to 30/6/2005	12,000
Year to 30/6/2006	18,000
Year to 30/6/2007	27,400

For the first tax year of the business (2004–05 which runs from 6 April 2004 until 5 April 2005) ACME is taxed on the profits from commencement at 1 July until the following 5 April:

$$9/12 \times 12,000 = \qquad £9,000$$

For the second tax year, the current-year basis applies and the first year's profit of £12,000 is subject to tax as this is the accounting period that ends in the next (second) tax year (2005–06):

Period to 30/6/05 = £12,000

For the third tax year, again the current-year basis applies and thus the next accounting period (to 30/6/2006) as it ends in the next tax year 2006–07:

Period to 30/6/06 = £18,000

If, later on, ACME ceases to trade, in the final tax year profits from the end of the basis period of the preceding year until the date of cessation are taxed. If ACME ceases on 30/8/2007, after the death of a key staff member, having made only £4,000 since the end of the previous period, the fourth tax year, on current-year basis and thus the next accounting period (to 30/6/07) plus the period to cessation is calculated together as it ends in the tax year 2007–08:

Period to 30/6/07 =	27,400
Plus period to cessation 30/8/07 =	4,000
	£31,400

PARTNERSHIPS

A partnership is treated as a separate entity for tax purposes and as such is required to submit a partnership return[38] showing business profits and

---

[37] ITTOIA 2005, ss 204–207 and 208–210.
[38] TMA 1970, ss 12AA–12AE.

the allocation of those profits between the partners. Each partnership is required to nominate a representative of the firm to be the point of contact for HMRC and ensure compliance but the authorities will act against any partner for liability and bind the others jointly and severally where this arrangement does not operate effectively for any reason. However, the partnership is not initially liable for tax on the profits allocated to the individual partners and each partner is responsible for reporting his own income and gains, including those derived from the partnership, in his own individual tax return. Special statutory elections can be made to allow partnerships to continue over long periods of time as individual partners retire or die and new ones join the firm, thus preventing the partnership being required to cease trading and recommence as a new entity at each change of personnel.[39]

Partnership and trustee returns

Partnership returns: in addition to the tax returns for individuals, a separate partnership return (Form SA 800) must be filed for partnerships, including a "partnership statement", containing the names, addresses and tax references of each partner, together with their share of profits, losses, charges on income, tax deducted at source etc.

Trustee returns: a separate trust and estate tax return (Form SA 900) must be filed by trustees to establish the tax liabilities on any income and gains chargeable on them and on certain settlers and beneficiaries.

LAND AND INCOME FROM PROPERTY

ITTOIA 2005, Pt 3 charges to tax all profits of a business letting property, which includes furnished and unfurnished lettings and certain lease premiums. The charge was previously under Sch A to ICTA 1988 and has a long history of over-complexity in the UK tax system[40] which has now been greatly simplified in the recent changes. In ITTOIA 2005, s 264 states that "a person's UK property business consists of every business which a person carries on for generating income from land in the United Kingdom and every transaction which the person enters into for that purpose".

---

[39] ICTA 1988, ss 113 as amended.
[40] See for example the idea of earned and unearned income; *Koenigsberger* v *Mellor* (1995) "personal exertions".

Essential Facts

- ICTA 1988, s 1(1), as amended by ITEPA 2003 and ITTOIA 2005, lists eight heads of charge for income.

- Some of the Schedules to ICTA 1988 still apply in relation to arrangements for charges to income tax.

- The system of self-assessment introduced in 1996–97 transfers the responsibility for calculating and settling tax liabilities to the taxpayer.

- A taxpayer's income from all sources must be aggregated to make a computation of liability, while keeping each category of income separate.

- Certain permitted statutory deductions, allowances and reliefs are permitted to be set against the taxpayer's aggregated total income prior to applying income tax.

- Where an employee receives earnings, national insurance contributions have to be accounted for as a cost to both the employer and the employee.

- Different principles apply to the trading income of an individual in self-employment.

- The basis of assessment for taxation of trading profits is the year of assessment, ending in an accounting date which can be chosen by the taxpayer. The year of assessment need not coincide with the tax year.

- A partnership is treated as a separate entity for tax purposes and must submit a partnership return showing business profits and the allocation of those profits among the partners.

- In the UK, the concept of income is based on straightforward criteria:
  - that the sum involved should fall within one of the statutory heads of charge;
  - that it should be of a revenue nature and not capital;
  - that it should not be specifically exempted by statute.

- The Royal Commission on the Taxation of Profits and Income (1954) outlined a series of tests known as the "badges of trade" to determine what activity should be regarded as trading for tax purposes.

- Deductions from taxable profits must be incurred wholly and exclusively for the purposes of the trade.

Essential Cases

Moss Empires Ltd v IRC (1937): profits are income only if they possess a quality of recurrence.

IRC v Cock Russell & Co Ltd (1949): stock must be valued at the lower of its cost price and the market value, where the market value is that typically available in the particular business or trade.

Badges of trade

Subject-matter: Rutledge v IRC (1929): when 1 million toilet rolls were bought and sold for a considerable profit, this was considered trading because of the nature of the goods involved (trade goods, not investments).

Frequency: Pickford v Quirke (1927): a transaction being performed four times in a similar fashion is indicative of trading, whereas a single operation would not be considered so.

Circumstances: Hudson's Bay Co v Stevens (1909): occasional irregular transactions over a period of time do not constitute an organised trade.

Supplementary work: Cape Brandy Syndicate v IRC (1921): modification and enhancement of goods to improve marketability is indicative of trading.

Motive: Wisdom v Chamberlain (1968): where transactions are entered into with the intention of making a profit and this is the prime motivation, this constitutes trading.

Length of ownership: a very weak badge, with no specific case authority. Quick sale tends to denote trading, though this can be rebutted by the facts.

Deductions

Wholly and exclusively: **Mallalieu v Drummond (1983)**: where there is duality of purpose in incurring an expense and one purpose is not business related, the expense is not deductible.

Remoteness: **Strong & Co of Romsey v Woodifield (1906)**: the context of payments made by a business in relation to the business determines whether it is a deductible expense.

Cost of drawings: **Sharkey v Wernher (1956)**: goods disposed of other than in the normal course of business must be accounted for at market value.

7 CORPORATION TAX

Corporation tax was introduced in April 1965, prior to which companies paid income tax like individuals and were treated as another category of legal person, able to accumulate income from a variety of sources and to make investments. However, corporation tax includes profits and gains of a capital nature in its charge to tax and as such companies and other non-incorporated associations liable to corporation tax do not pay capital gains tax. All UK-resident companies are liable to corporation tax, as are non-resident companies carrying on a trade in the UK through a UK permanent establishment[1] and clubs, societies and voluntary bodies (non-incorporated associations). A corporate body is considered resident in the UK if it is incorporated in the UK or if it is managed and controlled from the UK.[2]

The changes to the classification of income tax under ITTOIA 2005 did not affect company taxation; however, the introduction of a new bespoke Act in 2009 did. The Corporation Tax Act 2009 (CTA 2009) rewrites the corporation tax legislation dealing with trading, property and miscellaneous income and received Royal Assent on 26 March 2009; it applies to accounting periods commencing on or after 1 April 2009. Under this new legislation, companies are no longer taxed by reference to the old Sch D Cases I, III, V and VI of ICTA 1988, but are taxed on different types of income under new provisions which mirror the modern style of ITTOIA 2005, on the full amount of profits and gains arising in the relevant accounting period.[3]

Corporation tax is charged on accounting periods which are usually 12 months long and on the basis of company self-assessment returns, Forms CT600, lodged with HMRC in much the same way and on similar timescales to the returns lodged by individual taxpayers.[4] The corporation tax self-assessment scheme (CTSA), introduced with effect from April 1999, places the same legal burden upon officials and directors for tax compliance, as representatives of corporate entities, as is placed on individuals for personal tax liabilities.

---

[1] For definition of a permanent establishment, see Pt 1, Ch 1.
[2] FA 1988, s 66.
[3] Corporation Tax Act 2009, s 8(5).
[4] For details of the accounting period variations and the details of the corporation tax self-assessment scheme, see FA 1998, Sch 18, paras 2–7 and FA 2004, s 55.

SELF-ASSESSMENT SUMMARY

The CTSA regime was introduced for company accounting periods ending after 30 June 1999. The important CTSA features to note are:

- corporation tax returns must include a self-assessment based on the information in the return, taking account of reliefs and specifying the tax due for the period. This extends to tax payable on loans to participators and on profits of controlled foreign companies;
- the self-assessment creates the charge to tax without any action being required by HM Revenue & Customs (HMRC). Unless HMRC enquires into a return, the company's tax position will normally be regarded as finalised 12 months after the filing date for the return;
- companies are required to maintain and retain sufficient records to enable them to make a complete and correct return. Failure to maintain and keep records will give rise to penalties;

Unlike individuals, companies are usually charged tax at a single rate on their profits and gains and have no personal allowances to set against chargeable profits. The rate of tax is determined by reference to the level of corporate "profits for corporation tax purposes" (PFCTP) which includes all profits and capital gains plus dividends received from other UK companies that are not in the same corporate group. In the case of dividends, these must be "grossed up" at 100/90 before inclusion in the taxable computation figure.[5]

Corporation tax is payable in three banded rates and the thresholds for rates are based on 12-month accounting periods with *pro rata* apportionment of shorter or longer accounting periods, or where companies trade as a group to remove artificial advantages of splitting large corporations into small units. Thus, where tax is charged on a tax year basis (12 months) and a company has a 15-month accounting period, a 12/15 fraction will be applied to find the taxable profits for the given tax year. The marginal relief bands which sit between the rate bands provide a transition adjustment for growing companies faced with the tax consequences of that growth by mitigating the sudden jump in tax rates.

---

[5] ICTA 1988, ss 13 and 13AA.

Marginal relief is calculated as follows:

For FY 2009 the CT rates are 21 per cent for small companies and 28 per cent for large companies

Tax @ 21% on £300,000	=	£63,000
Tax @ 28% on £1,500,000	=	£420,000
Shortfall in tax (420,000–63,000)	=	£357,000

Thus £357,000 must be raised by the exchequer on profits falling in the "margin" between the two taxing zones for companies, from the £1,200,000 margin within that zone:

$$\frac{357,000}{1,200,000} \times 100 = 29.75$$

This results in a marginal rate of 29.75% on profits between £300,000 and £1.5 million. The marginal relief "fraction" used by the Treasury to work out this percentage is 7/400 for 2010–11.

In order to calculate the corporation tax payable, certain steps must be undertaken:

(1) determine the accounting period to be assessed;
(2) adjust the income for tax purposes and set off allowable expenditure for the period;
(3) add any chargeable gains and any income from received dividends;
(4) calculate the profits chargeable to corporation tax (PCTCP);
(5) apply the appropriate rate and apply any marginal relief.

Example: ACME Ltd

Allan, Craig and Morrice Enterprises (ACME Ltd) has a trading year from 1 January to 31 December in each year. The following is a calculation of corporation tax for the year ended 31 December 2008. This period straddles two financial years: 3 months in FY 2007 (January to March 2008) and 9 months in FY 2008 (April to December 2008).

	£	£
Net business profit		1,654,000
Add: Entertaining	3,000	
Depreciation	97,000	
Commission	42,000	
Fees	8,000	150,000
		1,804,000
Less: Plant and machinery allowance	61,000	
Lease premium allowance	3,000	64,000
		1,740,000
Trading profit		1,740,000
Interest on loans (Sch D, Case III)		2,100
Income from property (Sch A)		7,900
Chargeable gains		50,000
PCTCP (Chargeable profit)		1,800,000
FY 2004 @ 30% (on ¼) x 450,000 =		135,000
FY 2005 @ 30% (on ¾) x 1,350,000 =		378,000
Tax payable		513,000

Rules were introduced by FA 2002 to deal with intangible assets, which means intellectual property such as patents, copyrights, trademarks and goodwill. Companies can now claim an allowance for depreciation of such assets at a rate of 4 per cent per year. This is distinct from the usual rate of capital allowances on such items as plant and machinery and buildings. This regime was overhauled by the new Act in 2009 and intangible assets are now outwith the scope of corporation tax on chargeable gains.[6]

DISTRIBUTIONS

The term "distribution" is widely defined and effectively includes all methods of transferring a company's profits or assets to its members, the

---

[6] CTA 2009, Pt 8 (FA 2002, Sch 29).

shareholders, including the most common method which is by way of a dividend on each share held. For the company, distributions are made out of taxed income and are thus not deductible in arriving at its profit figure for a financial year. For individual shareholders the gross amount of the distribution is treated as income under ITTOIA 2005, Pt 4; for corporate shareholders the income is known as franked investment income. Franked investment income (FII) is the term applied to dividend income a company receives from its investment in other UK company shares. It is quite usual for companies to buy each other's shares, not only because of a common interest through shareholders or common projects, but purely at arm's length as an investment decision in order to make a return on money. The term "franked" relates to the fact that these dividends have already had tax at 10 per cent deducted by the paying company and hold a tax credit accordingly. Such payments are not included in the PCTCT calculation for this reason, but are included when determining the overall rate of corporation tax to be paid on the balance of profits and will affect the calculation of marginal relief. Thus to calculate corporation tax for a company that receives UK dividends, the "total profits from all sources" figure should be used, including FII to decide the rate of tax which will apply, but the PCTCT is the figure to which that rate is applied, excluding the FII.

Example: ACME Ltd

ACME Ltd has only £35,000 PCTCT but has FII of £30,000; therefore, although £35,000 is chargeable it will be charged at 21 per cent as the total profit is over £50,000 and this will affect the marginal rate calculation.

CAPITAL GAINS FOR COMPANIES

A company's chargeable gains are calculated in the same way as those of an individual. The definition of assets and the circumstances and occasions of disposals are the same as for individuals. No annual exemption is available to companies; neither is there taper relief on disposals of business assets. However, special rules exist for the disposal by one company of shareholdings in another.[7] Disposals among companies in the same corporate group are generally treated as "no gain, no loss" situations until the asset is disposed of outwith the group, and similar arrangements are in place with regard to losses and their use by members that are connected or within a group.

---

[7] TCGA 1992, Sch 7AC.

Example: connected companies

Ingrid owns 100 per cent of Hengist Ltd and her husband Thor owns 60 per cent of Horsa Ltd. The companies are connected companies because Ingrid is connected to Thor as his spouse.

Horsa Ltd subscribed for 10,000 £1 shares in Maxi Ltd in 2001. It sold this holding to Hengist Ltd in 2008 for £4,000, the market value at that time. The loss of £6,000 can only be used by Horsa Ltd against a gain arising in a deal with Hengist Ltd when they are connected persons for capital gains purposes.

Essential Facts

- Companies pay corporation tax on profits and gains of a capital nature.

- All UK-resident companies are liable to UK corporation tax, as are non-resident companies carrying on a trade in the UK through a UK permanent establishment and clubs, societies or voluntary bodies.

- Corporation tax is charged on accounting periods which are usually 12 months long and on the basis of self-assessment forms, in much the same way as the system for individual taxpayers.

- The rate of corporation tax is determined by reference to the level of corporate "profits for corporation tax purposes".

- Distributions are not deductible in arriving at a company's profit figure for a financial year.

- A company's chargeable gains are calculated in the same way as those of an individual.

8 CAPITAL GAINS TAX

Capital gains tax (CGT) was introduced in the Finance Act 1965 and was subsequently consolidated in the Capital Gains Tax Act 1979 (CGTA 1979) and most recently in the Taxation of Chargeable Gains Act 1992 (TCGA 1992). It was originally intended to tax profits on the disposal of a capital asset which were previously left untouched by a charge to income tax, in an effort to introduce equity to the direct tax system of the UK.

Persons liable to CGT include individuals, trustees and personal representatives, who are resident or ordinarily resident in the UK during any part of a year of assessment, and liability is on gains on the disposal of assets wherever such assets are situated. Companies are not liable to CGT and instead pay corporation tax on their chargeable gains. The rules for residence and domicile as discussed in Chapter 10 apply to CGT in the same way as they do to income tax. Non-residents are chargeable on gains arising from the disposal of UK assets only, and a non-UK domiciled individual (whether resident or not) is only liable to CGT where the gain is remitted to the UK. Chargeable gains arise on the disposal of assets and tax is charged on the net total of chargeable gains in a given year of assessment after the deduction of capital losses, taper relief and the annual exemption for capital gains.[1] The terms "asset" and "disposal" are not specifically defined in the legislation but a wide scope has been given to their respective meanings by the courts. All forms of property can be assets and are so for CGT purposes unless specifically exempted or excluded,[2] and a disposal, in its natural meaning, takes place whenever an owner divests himself of rights in or interests over an asset. Statute does look at an extended meaning for disposals to cover specific situations of complexity and the idea of the "deemed disposal".[3]

For disposals on or after 6 April 2008, individual taxpayers pay CGT at a single rate of 18 per cent. Prior to that CGT was levied at the rate of income tax applicable to the taxpayer in the given period of assessment. Thus, if the individual had a high earning year and also had some disposals of capital assets, then he would pay CGT at 40 per cent. Historically, the flat rate system has had more longevity than the variable rate or the

---

[1] TCGA 1992, ss 1, 2 and 9–12.
[2] *Cottle* v *Coldicott* (1995) and also *O'Brien* v *Bensons Hosiery Holdings Ltd* (1979).
[3] TCGA 1992, ss 71–73.

marginal income tax rate, with 30 per cent applying as a single rate up until 1988 when variable rates came in on certain types of transaction. In the current political climate, with the election of a Conservative–Liberal Democrat coalition Government, we are unlikely to see a change away from the single rate system in the foreseeable future.[4]

Capital gain calculation

Finlay bought a holiday cottage in April 1993 for £40,000 and sold it in July 2006 for £120,000. Indexation allowance at 0.156 is due for the 5 years from April 1993 to April 1998. Taper relief is due at 30 per cent for a non-business asset held for 8 years from 6 April 1998, plus one bonus year as the asset was owned on 17 March 1998. Finlay has a capital loss brought forward of £7,000 but makes no other disposals in 2006–07. His chargeable gains are:

	£	£
Proceeds		120,000
Less: Cost	40,000	
Indexation allowance: £40,000 × 0.156	6,240	
		46,240
Net gain		73,760
Loss brought forward		7,000
Net gain before taper relief:		66,760
Taper relief: 35% × 68,760		24,066
Net gain before annual exemption		£42,694

ANNUAL EXEMPTION

The annual exemption is available to every taxpayer, including children. It is also available to the personal representatives of a deceased person in the year of death (in addition to the deceased's own exemption) and in the following two tax years.

RETURNS

A person liable to capital gains tax must notify HM Revenue & Customs within 6 months of the end of the tax year, by 5 October, if a self-assessment return has not already been received.

---

[4] May 2010.

The capital gains tax pages of the self-assessment tax return must be completed and delivered to HMRC by the later of:

- 31 January after the end of the tax year in which the gain was made: or
- 3 months beginning with the date of a notice to complete the return.

The capital gains pages must be completed if an individual's chargeable gains *after* taper relief (or, if allowable losses are deductible, *before* those losses and taper relief) exceed the annual exemption, or if chargeable disposal proceeds exceed four times that exemption. The capital gains pages are also required if allowable losses or capital gains tax relief are being claimed, or an election is being made. There are corresponding rules for trustees and personal representatives.

The taxpayer is required to self-assess the capital gains tax liability. However, HM Revenue & Customs will calculate the liability where the return is delivered on or before 30 September following the year of assessment.

PAYMENT OF TAX

The payment rules for capital gains tax are the same as for income tax except that there are no payments on account and the tax is due on 31 January following the end of the year of assessment.

If consideration for the disposal of an asset is payable by instalments following the disposal for a period exceeding 18 months, the taxpayer can apply to pay the tax by instalments over a period not exceeding 8 years.

Capital gains tax on gifts of certain assets (and on certain deemed transfers involving settled property) may, by written election, be paid by 10 equal annual instalments, commencing from the normal due date, where the necessary conditions are satisfied.

Tax on chargeable gains may be recovered other than from the taxpayer on:

- disposals by gift;
- disposals by companies where the shareholder receives a capital distribution;
- disposals by group company members, and unpaid tax of former group members;

- disposals by companies in a scheme of reconstruction;
- the emigration of the donee following a gift relief claim.

The person from whom tax is recovered normally has right of recovery from the person originally assessed.

Example: arm's length bargain

Rowan has a holiday cottage which he needs to sell quickly to provide funds to save his business which is in trouble. He receives only one offer for the property, at a price 25 per cent lower than the asking price. Rowan accepts this offer and has made the best deal he can at that time, so the bargain is made at arm's length.[5]

CONNECTED PERSONS

Disposals between connected persons are always treated in the capital gains calculation as being made at market value. This applies regardless of the value of any actual consideration, or whether the bargain was struck on arm's-length terms.

The following are defined as "connected persons":

Individuals

An individual is connected with a spouse, close relatives (ie brothers, sisters, ancestors and other lineal descendants) and those relatives' spouses. Separated spouses remain connected, even if they are not "living together", until a decree absolute has been granted.

Trusts

A trustee is connected with the settlor of the trust, any person connected with the settlor, and any body corporate connected with the trust.

Partners

A partner is generally connected with other partners in partnership, together with their spouses and relatives.

Companies

A company is connected with other companies under common control, and with the persons controlling them.

---

[5] TCGA 1992, ss 272 and 286.

Example: connected persons transaction

In October 2002 sisters Ingrid and Astrid inherited from their parents paintings valued for inheritance tax at £10,000 each. In September 2005, they swap items on grounds of personal taste. However, the paintings have altered in value because of the artists' popularity (Ingrid's is worth £12,000 but Astrid's is worth £18,000). The sisters are connected parties so the consideration is taken to be the market value of the asset received in return.

Disposal by Ingrid

	£
Deemed disposal proceeds	12,000
Less Cost (agreed value for IHT)	10,000
Chargeable gain	£2,000

Disposal by Astrid

	£
Deemed disposal proceeds	18,000
Less Cost (agreed value for IHT)	10,000
Chargeable gain	£8,000

There is no taper relief due as the paintings are non-business assets that have been held for less than 3 years.

HUSBAND AND WIFE

Although spouses are connected persons until they are divorced, market value is not used to replace the consideration for transactions between a husband and wife who are living together. To be "living together" the couple do not have to be physically living in the same house. They must be married but not permanently separated by agreement, or separated under a court order. Transfers between spouses who are living together are treated as made on a "no gain, no loss" basis for capital gains tax purposes. However, if the asset is trading stock, the transfer is deemed to be at open market value.

To calculate the amount of taper relief due where an asset has been transferred between spouses who are married and living together, the ownership periods of both spouses are combined. However, whether the asset is treated as a business or non-business asset for taper relief will be determined as indicated by the method in IHTA 1984.

INDEXATION ALLOWANCE

Indexation allowance is an adjustment to reflect the effects of inflation on the cost of the asset. The allowance is calculated based on changes in the retail price index, and is applied separately to each item of allowable expenditure included in the calculation of a chargeable gain.[6]

For individuals (and also trustees and personal representatives), indexation allowance is calculated only for periods during which the asset was owned between 31 March 1982 and 5 April 1998. Taper relief applies instead to gains arising on assets disposed of after 5 April 1998. Indexation allowance is deducted in the capital gain calculation before the taper relief can reduce any net gain. The indexation allowance may reduce or extinguish a chargeable gain, but it cannot create a loss, or turn an unindexed gain into a capital loss.

Indexation allowance is calculated on the higher of an asset's original cost or its market value on 31 March 1982 (if the cost was incurred prior to that date) unless a rebasing election is in effect (see below), in which case indexation is calculated solely by reference to the asset's market value at 31 March 1982.

Indexation allowance continues to apply to chargeable gains made by companies beyond 5 April 1998. Taper relief does not apply for corporation tax purposes.

ASSETS HELD ON 31 MARCH 1982

Rebasing

Where an asset was acquired before 1 April 1982, the cost of the asset is replaced with its market value on 31 March 1982 in the capital gains computation. The owner is deemed to have disposed of and immediately reacquired all assets held on 31 March 1982 at their market value on that date. This is known as "rebasing".[7]

If a rebasing election is not made, separate computations will be required, both with and without rebasing, in which case the following rules apply:

- where it produces a larger indexed gain, then the gain without rebasing applies; or
- where it produces a larger loss, then the loss without rebasing applies; or

---

[6] TCGA 1992, ss 53–57.
[7] TCGA 1992, s 35.

- where it produces a gain, and a loss arises without rebasing (or vice versa), in which case the disposal is treated on a "no gain, no loss" basis; or

- in certain other cases a "no gain, no loss" basis (eg disposals between spouses, transfers of assets between group companies, gifts to charities etc).

In each case the indexation allowance is calculated on the higher of market value on 31 March 1982 and the original cost.

Election for universal rebasing

An irrevocable election can be made to HM Revenue & Customs to disapply the above restrictions in rebasing. The effect of this election is that gains and losses on disposals of assets held on 31 March 1982 are automatically calculated by reference to their market value at that date in all cases, irrespective of the gain or loss without rebasing. It also applies to the calculation of indexation allowance.

The election is irrevocable, and does not apply to items such as plant and machinery on which capital allowances could have been claimed. The time limit for making the election is:

- for capital gains tax purposes – 1 year from 31 January following the tax year in which the first disposal takes place;

- for corporation tax purposes – within 2 years after the accounting period in which the first disposal takes place; or

- at any later period allowed by HRMC.

The individual members of a group of companies cannot each make a rebasing election. The election must be made once only by the principal member of the group, to cover the group as a whole.

TAPER RELIEF

Prior to April 2008 and the new single rate regime for CGT, taper relief applied to individuals, trustees and personal representatives, but not companies. It reduced chargeable gains according to the number of whole years for which the asset has been held after 5 April 1998.[8]

Taper relief replaced indexation allowance, which continues to be available up to April 1998, but not for subsequent periods. However,

---

[8] TCGA 1992, s 2A; amended by FA 2000 and FA 2003.

companies continue receiving indexation allowance in respect of gains after 5 April 1998.

The relief reduces (tapers) chargeable gains according to the period of ownership of an asset, with more generous reductions for disposals of *business* assets than for *non-business* assets (see example below).

Where a *non-business* asset was acquired before 17 March 1998, a "bonus" year of taper relief is available. For example, a non-business asset acquired on 16 March 1998 and sold on 30 April 2005 will qualify for 8 years' taper relief (ie 7 complete years of ownership after 5 April 1998, plus the bonus year).

BUSINESS ASSETS

Business assets attract maximum taper relief of 75% after 2 years (4 years for disposals before 6 April 2002), leaving only 25 per cent subject to CGT. This equates to an effective tax rate of 10 per cent for a higher rate individual taxpayer or 5 per cent for a basic rate taxpayer. For trustees and personal representatives, the effective tax rate is 10 per cent.

The higher taper relief rates for business assets apply to the following:

- assets used in a trade carried on by the individual (either alone or in partnership). For disposals from 6 April 2004, the relief is extended to an asset used in a trade carried on by *any* individual, or by *any* partnership whose members include an individual;
- assets used in a trade carried on by the individual's "qualifying company" (see below);
- assets used in a trade carried on by a trading group company, if the holding company is the individual's "qualifying company";
- assets used in an office or employment with a person carrying on a trade; or
- shares in a "qualifying company".

In addition, for disposals from 6 April 2004, the higher taper relief applies to assets used in a trade carried on by a partnership whose members include the individual's "qualifying company", or by a trading group company if the holding company is the individual's "qualifying company".

NON-BUSINESS ASSETS

Non-business assets are defined as all assets other than business assets. They are treated less favourably than business assets, receiving no taper relief until year 3 of a 10-year maximum holding period. The rate of relief thereafter is 5 per cent per annum. A taxable gain may therefore be reduced by a maximum of 40 per cent, leaving 60 per cent subject to capital gains tax. The effective tax rates after full taper relief for individual higher rate and basic rate taxpayers are 24 per cent and 12 per cent respectively. The effective tax rate for trustees and personal representatives is 24 per cent.

THE NEW REGIME – ENTREPRENEURS' RELIEF

Entrepreneurs' relief represents a return to a more traditional view of CGT reliefs that were best exemplified in the former "retirement relief" which disappeared in 2003. From 6 April 2008,[9] entrepreneurs' relief (ER) applies to gains made on the disposal of all or part of a business or gains made on the disposal of assets following the cessation of a business, where these gains are made by persons involved in running the business. The first £1 million of gains that qualify for ER will be charged at an effective rate for CGT of 10 per cent rather than the new standard rate of 18 per cent, which will apply to all gains in excess of the £1 million threshold. The threshold is a lifetime ceiling for all business gains and can be applied to either one single claim or a series of successive claims. ER will not apply to members of approved employee share option schemes or company SIPs[10] unless the participants own more than 5 per cent of the business assets. In effect, in simple terms ER means a total of £80,000 in CGT relief potentially for each individual involved in the acquisition and disposal of business assets over their lifetime. The definitions of what constitute qualifying assets are contained in amendments to the existing CGT legislation.[11] ER reduces the capital gain chargeable to tax by 4/9 leaving the remaining of 5/9 of the total available for other CGT relief such as holdover relief, or for losses, annual exemption etc.

Example: entrepreneurs' relief on a business asset

Horsa gave 30 per cent of the share in his company to his son Hengist in October 2009, making a gain based on the market valuation of £190,000. Horsa also made a loss on the disposal of quoted business shares of £100,000 in May of the same year.

---

[9] FA 2008, Sch 3.
[10] Self-invested pension.
[11] TCGA 1992, ss 169N–169S.

	£
Gain on gift	190,000
ER @ 4/9 x 190,000	(84,444)
Taxable gain	105,556
Less brought forward	100,000
Chargeable gain (covered by annual exemption)	5,556

Taper relief example for comparison

Max bought a shop in April 1996 for £20,000 which is used in the partnership he runs with his wife. He sells the shop in September 2005 for £60,000. He makes no other disposals in 2005–06. The indexation factor from date of acquisition to April 1998 is 0.066.

At the time of disposal the asset has been held for 7 complete years after 5 April 1998, and has been used as a business asset for the whole of that period.

	£
Proceeds	60,000
Less Cost of acquisition	20,000
Unindexed gain	40,000
Indexation to April 1998 £20,000 x 0.066	1,320
Chargeable gain	38,680
Less Taper relief £38,680 x 75%	29,010
Taxable gain subject to annual exemption	£9,670

The fact that Max receives rent from the partnership for the shop makes no difference to the availability of taper relief on the disposal.

WASTING ASSETS

A wasting asset is one with a predictable useful life not exceeding 50 years. If it is a wasting chattel (personal possessions such as a TV) it is exempt from CGT. If it is an item of plant or machinery subject to capital allowances, there are specific rules on disposals calculated in proportion to the lifespan of the asset.[12] The main types of asset involved are certain

---

[12] TCGA 1992, ss 44–47.

varieties of time-limited options, patent rights, copyrights and leases. It is assumed for the calculation that the wasting asset reduces in value over its lifespan at a uniform rate in the same way as is done for a capital allowance, and the acquisition cost is reduced accordingly.

PART DISPOSALS

Where only part of an asset is disposed of it is necessary to calculate the original cost of the part sold before any gain can be computed on the disposal value.[13] The formula used for this calculation is as follows:

$$C \times \frac{A}{A + B}$$

where C is all the deductible expenditure on the whole asset; A is the sale proceeds on the part sold; and B is the market value of the part retained.

Example: part disposal

20 acres of farmland were bought in February 1991 for £20,000 and 8 acres of it were then sold in June 2006 for £24,000. The remainder of the land was worth £48,000 at the time of sale. Indexation factor is 0.360

$$20,000 \times \frac{24,000}{(24,000 + 48,000)} = £6,666$$

Indexation is therefore £6,666 x 0.360 = £2,400

Sale proceeds	£24,000	
Less		
Acquisition cost	£8,000	
Indexation	£2,400	£10,400
Gain		£13,600

Taper relief may be added to further reduce the gain if the land was a business asset.

MAIN RESIDENCE

An individual's sole or main residence (for CGT this is called the principal private residence (PPR)) is exempt from capital gains tax to the extent that

---

[13] TCGA 1992, s 42.

the owner has occupied it during the period of ownership and excluding any portion of the property used as a business asset.[14] Periods of actual or deemed occupation are:

- any absences totalling up to 3 years;
- any periods of employment-related absence abroad;
- any periods of up to 4 years when employment in the UK caused absence.

Each period of absence should be followed by a period of occupation to apply the rules strictly; however, the HMRC tends to take a lenient view, as an extra-statutory concession, where work-related absence of any kind is involved. The last 36 months of ownership are deemed occupation. Simple apportionment is used to determine how much of the period of ownership is exempt from tax and a similar method is used for non-qualifying portions of the property in relation to business use.

Example: main residence

William buys a house in Stonehaven in May 1983, for £45,000. He is a self-employed consultant, building up his client base, and uses one of the five apartments of his house as an office for his business. He occupies the house until 1 July 1985 when he had to work in London. His house was let until he returned on 31 March 1989. On 30 April 1994, because of increasing workloads in Europe, he left for the continent, returning on 1 May 1999 when he moved in with his girlfriend in Aberdeen. The house was eventually sold on 30 December 2005 for £220,000. William paid fees and costs of £5,000 on the sale.

May 1983 to July 1985	27 months	occupied	exempt
July 1985 to March 1989	45 months	working away in UK	exempt
March 1989 to April 1994	61 months	occupied	exempt
May 1994 to Dec 2002	104 months	not occupied	chargeable
Jan 2003 to Dec 2005	last 36 months	deemed occupied	exempt

In total, out of 273 months, 169 months are deemed occupied and 104 are not, the latter because upon William's return from the work-related absence the property was not re-occupied. Indexation factor from May 1983 to April 1998 (end of such allowance) is 0.929.

Calculation:

	£
Gross proceeds	220,000
Fees and costs	(5,000)
Net proceeds	215,000

---

[14] TCGA 1992, ss 222–226.

Less		
Acquisition cost		(45,000)
Unindexed/untapered gain		170,000
Indexation (0.929 x 45,000)		(41,800)
		128,200
PPR exemption (169/273 x 128,200)	79,362	
Less 1/5 for business use of house	(15,872)	
Net PPR exemption		(63,490)
INDEXED GAIN		64,710
Less Taper relief at 70%		(45,297)
CHARGEABLE GAIN		£19,413

BUSINESS RELIEFS

Various CGT reliefs relate to businesses, with the aim of encouraging business continuity and growth, unhindered by the prospect of taxation on sale or transfer, while the business continues to trade as a live asset, a going concern. This regime of relief is also to encourage a business to reinvest money in other businesses or Government-sponsored business incentive schemes,[15] rather than to take the money, as a gain, out of the economy. The three most notable examples of this are given below; however, for further examples of such reliefs, see TCGA 1992, ss 247, 135–137 and FA 2002, Sch 29.

Roll-over (replacement of business assets): TCGA 1992, ss 152–159

Where business assets are sold and the proceeds invested in another business asset, the gain on the disposal can be "rolled-over" and deducted from the cost of the new asset, thus postponing any taxable gain until the disposal of the newly acquired asset. The new asset must be bought within 1 year before and 3 years after the disposal of the old asset, and must be used for business purposes. The list of approved assets is contained in s 155 of the statute.

---

[15] Examples of these include: Enterprise Investment Scheme (EIS) and Venture Capital Trusts (VCT); see TCGA 1992, ss 150A and 150B.

Example: roll-over

Karen makes a gain of £50,000 on sale of machinery but buys new equipment for £90,000; she can roll her gain into the purchase, reducing it to £40,000 (£90,000 – £50,000). Thus, in any future disposal the acquisition cost of the new asset is lowered to take account of the rolled-over gain, thus widening the gap to the eventual future disposal. In this way the CGT is deferred rather than exempted. (Taper relief may also be available on future disposal.)

Hold-over relief (gifts of business assets): TCGA 1992, ss 165–169

This is a situation where a disposal by an individual (or trustees in certain cases) is *otherwise than a bargain at arm's length*, and therefore includes both gifts of assets and sales at undervalue. The recipient can be any "person" which in this situation can include a trust or a company. Any asset can be involved provided it is used in the relevant business as part of that business. The purpose of the relief is to allow for a situation where those in receipt of the gifted or undervalued assets were unable to pay the market price and the donor does not wish to pay the CGT. The alternative to this route would be the dissolution of the trade. The relief will be given only where a valid election is submitted by both transferor and transferee and for the purposes of both parties to the transfer the market value is used. The donor is disposing and the donee acquiring the business assets at their market value excluding the chargeable gain which is held over. The tax is postponed until the donee disposes of the asset or makes a further election to transfer on again. HMRC will normally insist on valuations of the assets at the time of transfer.

Example: hold-over

In 2006, Karen gives her software engineering business to her children, to run as a partnership. On a joint election under s 165 by the children as partners and Karen as donor, the CGT on the disposal is held over until any subsequent disposal by the children.

Incorporation relief: TCGA 1992, ss 162 and 162A

Subject to the new measures announced under entrepreneurs' relief outlined above, this takes the form of a postponement rather than an exemption from tax. Where an unincorporated business is disposed of to a company, any gains made on the disposal of chargeable business assets will be deducted from the value of the shares received. Thus, the gain is "rolled" into the share value, which must reflect the market value of the assets acquired, and therefore the gain will fall chargeable it and when the shares are disposed of and the business sold on. To qualify for the relief, the business must be transferred as a going concern, and all the assets must be included in the acquisition by the company.

Example: incorporation

Karen incorporates her business and sells it into a newly formed company in consideration for shares. There is a gain on the business assets of £50,000 and the market value of the shares is £200,000. The gain is rolled over into the shares so the acquisition cost of the shares becomes £150,000 (£200,000–£50,000) and the business assets are deemed acquired by the company at the market value of £200,000. Thus the gain is held over inside the company.

In addition to being disposals for CGT, gifts of assets may be chargeable to IHT, although some reliefs are available to offset this situation. For rules governing the interaction of CGT hold-over reliefs and IHT, and the implications for anti-avoidance, see TCGA 1992, s 260 and IHTA 1984, s 165. When chargeable gains are held over the transferee can add any IHT paid to the CGT acquisition cost to help offset a double charge.

Essential Facts

- Capital gains tax was introduced in the Finance Act 1965 and was consolidated in the Capital Gains Tax Act 1979 and the Taxation of Chargeable Gains Act 1992.
- Persons liable to capital gains tax include individuals, trustees and personal representatives, who are resident or ordinarily resident in the UK during any part of a year of assessment, and liability is on gains on the disposal of assets wherever they may be situated.
- The annual exemption is available to every taxpayer, including children.
- A person liable to capital gains tax must notify HMRC within 6 months of the end of the tax year if a self-assessment return has not already been received.
- Tax on chargeable gains may be recovered other than from the taxpayer, in certain situations.

- Disposals between connected persons are always treated as being made at market value, regardless of any actual consideration, except in the case of spouses, whose transactions are treated as made on a "no gain, no loss" basis.
- Indexation allowance is an adjustment to reflect the effects of inflation on the cost of the asset.
- Where an asset was acquired before 1 April 1982, the cost of the asset is replaced with its market value on 31 March 1982 in the capital gains tax computation.
- Taper relief affects individuals, trustees and personal representatives, but not companies. It reduces chargeable gains according to the number of whole years for which the asset has been held after 5 April 1998. It replaces indexation allowance, although companies continue receiving indexation allowance in respect of gains after that date.
- A wasting asset is one with a predictable useful life not exceeding 50 years.
- Where only part of an asset is disposed of, a formula is used to calculate the original cost of the part sold before any gain can be computed on the disposal value.
- Roll-over relief, hold-over relief and incorporation relief apply to business transfers.

9 INHERITANCE TAX

OUTLINE

Inheritance tax (IHT) was brought into effect by FA 1986 with effect from 31 March of that year. It replaced the existing capital transfer tax regime which in turn had replaced estate duty, and follows in a long line of measures to tax property transfers from estates. The governing statute is the Inheritance Tax Act 1984 (IHTA 1984), which taxes chargeable transfers made on death (*mortis causa*) or within 7 years before death (*inter vivos*). IHT is chargeable when a chargeable transfer is made by an individual and that transfer is not exempt.[1] A transfer of value is defined as any disposition which reduces the value of the transferor's estate; this includes certain deemed transfers such as the termination of an interest in possession in settled property or the writing-off of a debt, the failure to exercise a right or the destruction of an asset. Such transfers must be gratuitous and thus not normally commercial in nature or in return for a consideration. Chargeable transfers within the 7-year period ending with the latest transfer are cumulated for IHT purposes. Where total transfers do not exceed the "nil rate band" there is no IHT liability.

Examples of transfers of value

- William gives his house, worth £250,000, to his son, Finlay.
- Karen sells her car, worth £8,000, to her daughter, Ingrid, for £1,000.

Individuals who are domiciled in the UK are chargeable on their worldwide assets and non-UK domiciled individuals are liable on UK property only. Issues regarding domicile are dealt with in Chapter 10.

TYPES OF TRANSFER

In addition to the distinction between lifetime transfers and transfers on death, lifetime transfers are categorised as exempt, potentially exempt or chargeable on the following basis.

---

[1] IHTA 1984, s 2(1).

Exempt transfers

Under IHTA 1984 certain types of gifts are regarded as exempt. These include gifts between spouses, gifts to UK charities, gifts to political parties, gifts for national purposes and certain gifts for specified personal purposes such as on the occasion of marriage.[2] Transfers of value during a person's lifetime of up to £3,000 per tax year are exempt from IHT and any unused portion of this annual exemption can be carried forward for one year. Normal expenditure out of income is exempt if it can be shown that it was typical of the transferor's lifestyle and spending behaviour. Small gifts up to an annual value of £250 are exempt, and this applies to any number of individual small gifts of that value to separate persons and is in addition to the annual exemption of £3,000. Every person is, in the sense of liability to inheritance tax, an estate waiting to be realised and each estate is entitled to a one-off disregard known as the "nil rate band" (NRB). This has been a political football since the establishment of the current IHT regime as it places the tax as either potentially burdensome to many modestly wealthy persons or merely a concern for the very well-off, depending on the level at which it is set. The current level of £325,000 is now likely to rise significantly with the election of a Conservative-dominated Government.[3]

Potentially exempt transfers (PETs)

A PET is a transfer of value made by an individual which would otherwise be a chargeable transfer but which is made 7 years or more before the transferor's death; where the transferor dies within 7 years the PET becomes a chargeable transfer. PETs are gifts to individuals or a trust for the disabled.

Chargeable lifetime transfers (CLTs)

A CLT is a transfer made by an individual which is neither exempt nor potentially exempt: typically transfers into discretionary trusts or by members of a close company. These transfers are charged by reference to the cumulative total over a 7-year period, after which they fall out of charge. Tax is initially charged at the time of transfer at half the death rate, with further tax due if the transferor dies within the 7-year period. Where the transferor bears the IHT liability, the tax is a cost to the estate and thus the transfer must be grossed up to reflect the full reduction in the estate.

---

[2] IHTA 1984, ss 2, 3, 18–29A, 30–35A.
[3] General Election of 6 May 2010.

CUMULATION AND THE IHT THRESHOLD

Chargeable transfers within the 7-year period ending with the date of the latest chargeable transfer are cumulated, for the purposes of determining the IHT rate. Where total chargeable transfers do not exceed the "nil rate band" there is no IHT liability.

A person is treated as making a notional transfer of value of the whole estate immediately before his death, and IHT is charged accordingly. The tax charged on the estate depends on the aggregate chargeable lifetime transfers and potentially exempt transfers in the 7 years preceding death. The estate generally consists of all the property to which the individual was beneficially entitled, less excluded property and liabilities.

VALUATION OF ESTATE

The value of assets comprised in a person's estate is broadly their open market value immediately before death. However, death itself may affect property values, and any change in the value of the estate by reason of death is taken into account as if the change had occurred before death. Any changes in value resulting from additions to estate property as a consequence of death must also be taken into account (eg the proceeds from a life policy), except for:

- decreases in value of close company shares or securities resulting from alterations in (or rights attaching to) them;
- the termination on death of any interest; and
- the passing of any interest by survivorship.

Particular assets

- *Life policies*: The proceeds of a policy taken out on the person's own life or for his own benefit which are payable on death to the deceased's personal representatives are taken into account as part of the estate.
- *Quoted shares and securities*: The lower valuation is applied, using the following methods, based on capital gains tax valuation rules:
  (i) the "quarter-up" method, ie the lower closing Stock Exchange price plus one-quarter of the difference between the lower and higher closing prices; or
  (ii) mid-price between the highest and lowest recorded bargains for the day of valuation.
- *Unquoted shares and securities*: The valuation is based on the price that the shares or securities might reasonably be expected to fetch when

sold in the open market if any prospective purchaser possessed all the information that might reasonably be required. In practice, the IHT value will be subject to negotiation with Shares Valuation, a specialist HMRC office. If a valuation cannot be agreed, it will be subject to appeal before the Special Commissioners and thereafter to the courts.

Example: lifetime transfers

Karen transfers £92,000 to a discretionary trust on 1 May 2005, £194,000 on 31 December 2005 and a further £35,000 on 1 February 2006. She bears the tax and she had made no other chargeable transfers. The inheritance tax position is as follows.

	£	£	£
Gift on 1 May 2005		92,000	
Deduct Annual exemption 2005–06	3,000		
Annual exemption 2004–05	3,000	6,000	
		86,000	
Covered by nil rate band of £275,000			
Gifts on 31 December 2005		194,000	
(*Note*: Annual exemption already used for 2005–06)			
Cumulative net transfers		£280,000	
Tax thereon			
£0–275,000		–	
£275,001–280,000 (£5,000 x ¼)		1,250	
Tax on gift		1,250	

Gift on 1 February 2005

	Gross	Tax	Net
Cumulative totals	281,250	1,250	280,000
Add: Latest net transfer of £35,000	43,750	8,750	35,000
	£325,000	£10,000	£315,000

Tax on £315,000	
£0–275,000	–
£275,001–315,000 (£40,000 x ¼)	10,000
	10,000
Deduct: Tax on previous transfers	1,250
Tax on latest gift	£8,750

PAYMENT OF TAX
CLTs

The transferor is primarily liable to IHT in respect of chargeable lifetime transfers. However, if IHT remains unpaid beyond the due date, it can become the liability of the following:

- the transferee:
- any person in whom the property is vested;
- any person who becomes beneficially entitled to an interest in possession of the property; or
- the beneficiary of a settlement (where the property was transferred to it) for whose benefit the property or its income is applied.

The above are also liable for additional IHT on chargeable transfers, in the event of the transferor's death within 7 years of making them. However, the deceased's personal representatives may become liable to the extent that the tax remains unpaid.

PETs

The IHT liability on PETs becoming chargeable upon the death of the transferor within 7 years is that of the transferee(s) and/or the deceased's personal representatives, as in lifetime transfers above.

Transfers on death

The persons liable in respect of transfers on death are:

- the deceased's personal representatives (generally in respect of property which was not settled before death);
- the trustees of a settlement (in respect of property settled before death);
- any person who becomes beneficially entitled to an interest in possession of the property;
- the beneficiary of a settlement (where the property was included in it at death) for whose benefit the property or its income is applied.

The IHT Direct Payment Scheme enables the personal representatives to draw on money held in the deceased's bank or building society accounts to pay the IHT due on delivery of the relevant return form.

Due dates for payment

Lifetime transfers (other than additional liability on death)

- Tax is usually due 6 months after the end of the month in which the transfer takes place.
- Tax due on a chargeable lifetime transfer made after 5 April and before 1 October in any year is due at the end of April in the following year.
- Tax may be payable before accounts are due to be rendered.

Exceptions

- Tax chargeable on the ending of conditional exemption for works of art, historic buildings etc, on woodlands and on maintenance funds for historic buildings is always payable 6 months after the end of the month in which the chargeable event occurs.

Transfers on death

- Tax is due 6 months after the end of the month in which death occurred.
- The personal representatives of a deceased's estate must pay any IHT due at the time of applying for probate.
- At the same time, they may pay any other tax on the death, at the request of the persons liable.

Lifetime transfers – additional liability on death

Where tax or additional tax is due at death because:

- a potentially exempt transfer proves to be a chargeable transfer; or
- the transferor dies within 7 years of making a chargeable lifetime transfer; or
- the settlor dies within 7 years of the transfer and a further liability arises under the rules relating to settlements without interests in possession,

the additional tax is due 6 months after the end of the month of death.

Payment by instalments

IHT may be paid by 10 equal yearly instalments on chargeable transfers of qualifying assets, in respect of the following:

- transfer made on death;

- chargeable lifetime transfers where the IHT is borne by the transferee;
- settled property remaining in the settlement;
- PETs becoming chargeable (but only where the transferee still holds qualifying property upon the transferor's death).

For these purposes, "qualifying assets" include:

(a) land of any description, wherever situated;

(b) controlling shareholdings;

(c) unquoted shares (and in certain cases securities), broadly where the deceased did not have a controlling interest immediately before death and:

- the tax cannot be paid without undue hardship; or
- their value exceeds £20,000, and the holding is at least 10 per cent; or
- for transfers on death, the tax payable on those shares and securities, together with other instalment assets, amounts to 20 per cent or more of the tax payable by that same person;

(d) a business or an interest in a business;

(e) woodlands.

The first instalment is payable on the normal due date for the whole tax, if it were not payable by instalments.

Interest is charged on instalments paid late. However, in certain cases (eg land which does not form part of a business, land not attracting agricultural property relief, or shares in an investment company), interest is charged on the total tax outstanding, and is added to each instalment.

If the instalment property is sold, the outstanding tax becomes payable immediately.

Post-death variation

It may well be that a will, though drawn up with the best intentions by the testator, does not best suit the intended beneficiaries with regard to either tax issues or appropriate disposition of the deceased's estate. It may therefore be in the interests of the beneficiaries to make changes to the will after death. Such changes are permitted if made within 2 years of death and are seen as taking effect as if provided for in the original will.[4]

---

4 IHTA 1984, s 142.

The changes must be made by a deed of variation (also known as a deed of family arrangement) which is agreed by all the beneficiaries.

Example: deed varying disposition on death

Arthur dies in December 2005, leaving his estate of £302,000 to his wife absolutely. His wife, having an index-linked widow's pension, agreed with her sons, Bob and Charlie, that they could benefit from the estate to the extent of £275,000 in equal shares, ie £137,500 each.

A deed of variation is duly executed, including a statement that the variation should apply for inheritance tax purposes. Arthur had made no chargeable transfers before his death.

	£
Exempt transfer to widow	27,000
Transfer to Bob	137,500
Transfer to Charlie	137,500
	275,000
IHT payable	—

TRANSFERS BETWEEN SPOUSES

Transfers of value between spouses are exempt from inheritance tax:

(a) where property becomes compromised in the transferee's estate, by the amount by which the transferor's estate is diminished, or

(b) in any other case (eg payment by the transferor of his spouse's debt), by the amount by which the transferee's estate is increased.

For these purposes, property is given to a person if it becomes his property or is held in trust for him.

If, immediately before the transfer, the transferor, but not the transferor's spouse, is domiciled in the UK the exemption is limited to a cumulative total of £55,000, without grossing-up for tax.

The Civil Partnership Act 2004 (CPA 2004), which gives legal recognition to same-sex couples, became law in November 2004. One of the key taxation areas that will be affected by this legislation is inheritance tax where, in future, transfers between partners will be exempt.

ANNUAL EXEMPTION AND NIL RATE BAND

Example

William, who has made no other transfers of value, made gifts to his brother of £15,000 on 1 July 2004 and £14,000 on 1 June 2005. William

dies on 1 October 2009, with an estate valued at £475,000.
Annual exemptions are available as follows:

2007–08	£	£
1 July 2007 gift		15,000
Deduct: 2007–08 annual exemption	3,000	
2006–06 annual exemption (part)	3,000	
		6,000
		9,000

2008–09	£
1 June 2008 gift	14,000
Deduct: 2008–09 annual exemption	3,000
PET becoming chargeable on death	£11,000

The PET, having become a chargeable transfer as a result of death within
7 years, is covered by the nil rate band but is aggregated with the death
estate in computing the IHT payable on death.

	£	£
Death estate		475,000
Residual PET		11,000
		486,000
Less: NRB	325,000	
Chargeable to tax		161,000
161,000@ 40% =		£64,400

BUSINESS PROPERTY RELIEF (BPR)

Automatic relief from IHT is available for transfers of "relevant business
property" where certain conditions are satisfied for:

- lifetime transfers;
- transfers on death; and
- relevant business property in a discretionary trust.

Transfers of value are reduced, without monetary limit, by specified
percentages depending upon the type of property.

For these purposes, "relevant business property" consists of:

- *a business or interest in a business*: sole traders and partnerships carrying on a profession or vocation for profit are eligible (although businesses dealing wholly or mainly in investments do not generally qualify);
- *shares or securities*: different rates of relief apply, depending on whether the shares are quoted or unquoted and the percentage of voting control held (but companies dealing wholly or mainly in investments do not generally qualify);
- *land, buildings, machinery or plant*: the asset must, immediately before the transfer, have been used wholly or mainly for the purposes of a qualifying business carried on by:
    - (i) a company controlled by the transferor; or
    - (ii) a business of which the transferor was then a partner; or
    - (iii) the transferor, if the property was settled property and he was beneficially entitled to an interest in possession in it.

The relief is not available unless the business, or the transferor's interest in it, or the company's shares or securities, are relevant business property; and the relief applies to transfers of the whole or part of a business, as opposed to business assets.

The transferor must normally have owned the relevant business property throughout the 2-year period prior to the transfer, unless it is replacement business property and the combined ownership period amounts to at least 2 out of the 5 years prior to the transfer. Property inherited on a spouse's death is deemed acquired when the deceased spouse acquired it. Otherwise, property is deemed acquired at the date of death.

Excepted assets

The value of relevant business property attributable to excepted assets does not qualify for BPR. "Excepted assets" include investments and excessive cash deposits held by businesses or companies which are not:

- used wholly or mainly for the business throughout the 2 years immediately preceding the transfer (or since acquisition, if earlier); or
- required at the time of transfer for future use in the business.

AGRICULTURAL PROPERTY RELIEF (APR)

Relief from IHT is available for transfers of agricultural property in the UK, Channel Islands and the Isle of Man, where certain conditions are satisfied. The rules are broadly similar to those for business property relief, in relation to:

- replacement property;
- binding contracts for sale; and
- periods for which the property must be held by the transferee.

The relief, which is automatic, reduces transfers of value by specified percentages and is available for transfers during lifetime, on death and involving the relevant property of a discretionary trust. The percentages are:

- vacant possession or right to
  obtain it within 12 months (or 24 months by concession)   100%
- entitled to 50% relief at 9 March 1981
  and from that date beneficially entitled to
  interests but without vacant possession rights   100%
- agricultural land let on tenancy starting
  after 31 August 1995   100%
- other transfers   50%

The agricultural value of agricultural property is taken as the value of the property if subject to a perpetual covenant prohibiting its use other than as agricultural property.

For these purposes, "agricultural property" consists of agricultural land or pasture, and includes woodlands or any buildings used in connection with the intensive rearing of livestock or fish (if occupied with the land, where the occupation is ancillary to that of the agricultural land or pasture). It also includes cottages, farm buildings and farmhouses, together with the land occupied by them, with a character appropriate to the property.

To qualify for the relief, the agricultural property must have been:

- occupied by the transferor for the purposes of agriculture throughout the 2 years ending with the date of transfer; or
- owned by the transferor throughout the period of 7 years ending with the date of transfer *and* occupied throughout that period (by him or otherwise) for the purposes of agriculture.

If the agricultural property replaced other agricultural property, the ownership requirement is satisfied if:

- the transferor occupied it and the replaced property for at least 2 out of the last 5 years; or
- the transferor owned the properties (which were occupied for agriculture by him or someone else) for at least 7 out of the last 10 years.

APR is given in priority to BPR. To the extent that a transfer does not qualify for APR, it may qualify for BPR instead if the conditions for that relief are satisfied.

QUICK SUCCESSION RELIEF

Relief for successive IHT charges is available where:

- there is a transfer of property, within 5 years of an earlier transfer which increased the transferor's estate; and
- the later transfer:
  (a) arises on death; or
  (b) is of settled property, and
      – the transferor was entitled to an interest in possession;
      – the earlier transfer was of the same property; and
      – the property was/became settled property on earlier transfer.

Where these conditions are satisfied, the tax charge on the later transfer is calculated in the normal way. The later IHT charge is reduced by a percentage of the tax charged on the original net receipt from the original transfer. The percentage varies according to the length of time between the dates of transfer and death.

ESSENTIAL FACTS

- Inheritance tax replaced the existing capital transfer tax regime which in turn had replaced estate duty.
- The governing statute is the Inheritance Tax Act 1984 which taxes chargeable transfers made on death or within 7 years before death.
- Lifetime transfers are categorised as exempt, potentially exempt or chargeable.
- Chargeable transfers within the 7-year period ending with the date of the latest chargeable transfer are cumulated, for the purposes of determining the IHT rate.
- The beneficiaries may make changes to the will after the testator's death. Such changes are permitted if made within 2 years of death and must be made by a deed of variation.
- Business property relief, agricultural property relief and quick succession relief are available.

10   THE INTERNATIONAL DIMENSION

OUTLINE

In international terms, tax law is a blend of the theoretical and the practical. Theoretically, a nation could impose tax on anyone anywhere; however, in practical terms to enforce such an imposition would be impossible.[1] The factors which determine whether an individual should become liable to the taxes imposed by a particular jurisdiction are residence, ordinary residence and domicile. As a rule, in terms of the UK, a UK-domiciled and UK-resident person is liable to income tax on all income, whatever its source, and a non-resident is liable only in respect of income arising in the UK. A non-domiciled UK resident individual is only liable for foreign income where it is remitted to the UK.

RESIDENCE AND DOMICILE IN THE UK

There is no statutory definition of "residence" and in practice great emphasis is placed on the HMRC code of practice.[2] This situation arises since the cases on which the code is based are illustrations of the principle that residence is a question of fact and thus Commissioners' decisions[3] cannot be reversed by the courts simply because the courts would not have reached the same conclusion. IR20 is based on decisions in favour of HMRC and does not dwell on those in favour of the taxpayers.

Residence and domicile are two distinct legal concepts. The key question for the UK tax system is in this context a substantive and practical one; whether a particular legal person is resident in the UK or not. In the context of conflict of laws, the question is: where does that legal person have a domicile? Thus, a legal person may have two residences or no residence but must have a domicile and can have only one domicile.

Residence

A person who is not present in the UK throughout an entire tax year can still be deemed resident;[4] this is a question of fact and open to

---

[1] For a discussion of tax collection and enforcement from a practical standpoint, see *Clark* v *Oceanic Contractors Inc* (1983).

[2] As contained in SP IR20.

[3] Commissioners for Revenue and Customs: the court of first instance in tax matters in the UK.

[4] *Reed* v *Clark* (1985).

determination.[5] A legal person may be held to be resident in the UK despite the absence of any desire or intention, and the courts will look at factors such as past history, present habits and frequency and duration of visits to the UK.[6] The following four rules are the basis of the judgment as to UK residence as outlined in IR20.

(1) 183-day rule: under ICTA 1988, s 336, a person who actually resides in the UK for a period equal in the whole to 6 months in any year of assessment is treated as resident.[7]

(2) Habitual and substantial visits: visitors are generally regarded as resident in the UK, after a pattern of visits over a period of 4 years which average 91 days per year is established as a matter of fact.[8]

(3) Available accommodation: some time ago, the Revenue regarded the holding of accommodation in the UK as evidence of actual residence; however, this is no longer the case, as the wider view expressed in ICTA 1988, ss 334–336 now establishes further criteria. However, owning or leasing accommodation indicates an intention to stay and is still relevant in acquiring or giving up residence.

(4) Arrival in the UK: an individual coming to the UK to work for at least 2 years will be treated as resident from the day of arrival until the day of departure. If the arrival is for an unknown period, the trigger for residence will be the 183-day rule as listed in item (1) above.

An individual who is resident and domiciled in the UK in a tax year is liable to tax on his worldwide income, whereas an individual who is not resident in the UK in a tax year is liable only on his income arising in the UK.

Example

Andreas comes to the UK from Germany to study law at Aberdeen University. Even though his LL.M. course will last only 1 year, from September 2009 till September 2010, he will trigger the 183-day rule and will be regarded as resident for tax purposes from the date of his arrival (ICTA 1988, s 336).

---

[5] ICTA 1988, s 334.

[6] *Levene* v *IRC* (1928); *Lysaght* v *IRC* (1928).

[7] *Wilkie* v *IRC* (1952) where the interpretation of the word "months" was discussed.

[8] *Levene* (1928); *Lysaght* (1928).

Domicile

Persons are domiciled where they have, or are deemed by law to have, their permanent home. This is the place of their birth (domicile of origin) unless otherwise established by the active selection of another domicile (domicile of choice). The onus of proof of the abandonment of the domicile of origin, in any dispute, is on those who seek to establish a domicile of choice. Very strong evidence of such a change is required.[9] It would be necessary to show that an individual has abandoned all ties with the country of original domicile and now considers the new country of chosen domicile to be "home". In *F and F v IRC* (2000), the court held that obtaining a British passport was not sufficient evidence of establishing a domicile of choice, as the individual, who was an Iranian, had expressed a desire to return to Iran in the future. A domicile of choice is less fundamental to an individual and can more readily be discarded or allowed to lapse than a domicile of origin, possibly resulting in the re-establishment of the domicile of origin.[10]

Married women do not automatically acquire the domicile of their husband upon marriage and hold their own domicile of origin unless or until they elect to adopt the domicile of their husband as a domicile of choice.

Children usually change domicile along with their parents, although the position may differ where the parents are deceased, separated or divorced. Any individual is capable of holding an independent domicile, based on birth or choice, when that individual attains the age of 16, irrespective of any alterations of domicile established for them as a result of parental decisions.

For the purposes of inheritance tax only, an individual can be deemed to be domiciled in the UK, even if not normally so regarded in terms of general law.[11] An individual can be deemed domiciled if he has:

(1) been resident in the UK for at least 17 of the last 20 tax years; or

(1) been regarded as domiciled in the UK at any time in the last 3 tax years.

(1) emigrated during the past 3 years (despite the position in general law).

---

[9] *AG v Coote* (1817), *Bell v Kennedy* (1868), *F and F v IRC* (2000) and *Surveyor v CIR* (2002).

[10] *Bell v Kennedy* (1868).

[11] IHTA 1984, s 267.

SUMMARY

(1) International tax law is an aggregate of the domestic tax law, insofar as that law applies to situations with a foreign connection, and international tax treaties, concluded primarily for the avoidance of double taxation.

(2) International tax treaties and customs usually prevail, when in conflict with domestic legislation.

(3) International tax law may provide for specific remedies and judicial procedures within underlying international agreements.

(4) The European Union is unique in that it has supranational law and related judicial procedures in operation for all 25 Member States of the Union.

(5) Most tax disputes with a foreign connection are tried by domestic courts within their respective jurisdiction and domestic courts generally decline enforcement of a foreign tax law, unless international obligations provide for such enforcement.[12]

Essential Facts

- A person who is not present in the UK throughout an entire tax year can still be deemed resident. A legal person may be held to be resident in the UK, despite the absence of any desire or intention. These questions are open to determination by examination of factors such as past history, present habits and frequency and duration of visits to the UK.

- The 183-day rule: a person who actually resides in the UK for a period equal in the whole to 6 months in any year of assessment is treated as resident.

- Persons are domiciled where they have, or are deemed by law to have, their permanent home.

---

[12] *Government of India v Taylor* (1956).

11 VALUE ADDED TAX

Value added tax (VAT) is largely a phenomenon of the last 50 years, and has spread rapidly throughout the developed world and is now increasingly being applied in the developing world. Now, all OECD members, with the exception of the USA, have adopted VAT systems and the EU regards VAT as a cornerstone of the establishment of European Economic Community on which the EU is based. VAT is distinctive in style from a sales tax in that it is administered and collected at each transaction stage of the commercial cycle – at each stage where some value is added – whereas a sales tax is collected only at point of sale to the final consumer. The starting point of VAT law is the sixth VAT Directive of the EEC which took effect from 1 January 1978, though VAT had existed in the UK since it had joined the EEC in 1973. The sixth Directive standardised VAT for all EEC members.[1] For reasons of rationalisation and clarification, the sixth VAT Directive was recast by Council Directive 2006/112 EC of 28 November 2006 ("the Recast Directive"), though this does not bring about material changes to existing legislation.[2] The cross-jurisdictional nature of VAT and its fundamental importance to the EU was reinforced by the European Court of Justice in its decision of July 2009, which signalled a position that simplifies the recovery of VAT in relation to expenditure incurred by a business operating through fixed establishments in other Member States. The ECJ ruled, in *Commission of the European Communities v Italian Republic* (2008), that, subject to national rules, a taxable person having a fixed establishment in one Member State is regarded as established in that Member State, and can apply for the deduction of the VAT incurred on purchases made in that Member State, whether the purchases are effected through its fixed establishment, or directly by its principal or head office establishment wherever established, ie in another EU Member State or outside the EU.

VAT is therefore a tax on transactions, which are the supply of goods or services made within a given jurisdiction by a taxable, non-exempt person. Goods can be defined as tangible property which is not money or land and the supply of goods is the transfer of ownership for a commercial

[1] Treaty of Rome, Art 189 makes the provisions of the sixth Directive mandatory for all EEC members. This is now covered by Art 113 of the Consolidated Version of the Treaty on the Functioning of the European Union.

[2] Council Directive 2006/112 EC.

consideration. The taxable value of the supply is normally the amount of the consideration or the market value equivalent. Supply of services in terms of VAT is a more esoteric matter, and a service can be anything done by a taxable person for a commercial consideration. Financial services are usually exempted in VAT systems because of the practical difficulty in ascertaining the actual consideration for a particular service, where money is in and of itself the key to the transaction. Additionally, VAT taxes and monitors the import and export of goods and services across jurisdictional borders.

The basic legislation in the UK is the Value Added Tax Act 1994 (VATA 1994), with many of the detailed rules contained in orders under statutory instruments made under s 97 of the 1994 Act. The HMRC is responsible for the collection and management of VAT[3] and appeals against its decisions lie with VAT tribunals[4] and thereafter in the mainstream courts, as with other tax appeals. Under EC law, the ECJ has jurisdiction to give rulings on legal interpretation referred to it by national courts and tribunals, including VAT tribunals,[5] and, at the top of our domestic legal tree, the UK Supreme Court is bound to refer a case if there is any doubt.

REGISTRATION REQUIREMENTS

Under VATA 1994, Sch 1, a taxable person must be registered for VAT if:

- at the end of any given month of trading the value of taxable supplies made over the previous 12 months exceeds £68,000 exclusive of VAT, with effect from 1 April 2009; or
- at any time there are reasonable grounds for believing that the value of the taxable supplies that he will make in the next 30 days will exceed £68,000, for the 12-month period, exclusive of VAT.

HMRC must be informed within 30 days of the end of the relevant month when the above conditions are deemed to apply. Additionally, a person who satisfies HMRC that pre-trading activities are being carried on with a view to making taxable supplies can register for VAT,[6] as can persons who have small businesses under the threshold but can justify registration

---

[3] VATA 1994, Sch 11, para 1.
[4] VATA 1994, s 83; and see Tribunals, Courts and Enforcement Act 2007.
[5] *Naturally Yours Cosmetics Ltd* v *C & E Comrs* (1988).
[6] *Merseyside Cablevision Ltd* v *C & E Comrs* (1987).

on a voluntary basis for reasons of cash flow. Failure to register not only causes the imposition of penalties for breach of the regulations but also causes the liability and registration to be backdated to the time when notification should have taken place.

VAT CHAIN

VAT is charged by the supplier and recovered by the customer at each stage of the commercial chain until the final consumer is reached who is not registered for VAT and thus pays the VAT cost and cannot offset this. VAT covers all commercial transactions, though not all are subject to the standard VAT rate.

VAT standard rate is 17.5 per cent in the UK. There is a reduced rate of 5 per cent for certain special items. Items classed as social goods[7] are zero-rated which means they are charged in the VAT chain but no tax is applied, so a trader charges no output tax on the item but is able to recover all input tax paid out. Exempt items are those which are excluded from the VAT system of charge, which, although reducing the cost to the consumer, does not help the trader who still has overhead costs which cannot be claimed back, as is the case with zero-rated supplies. Exempt items include financial products, insurance premiums and healthcare.

VAT BUSINESS

Supplies must be made in the course of a business[8] and a "business" is fairly loosely defined, in the tradition of the UK tax authorities, in s 47 of VATA 1994 as including "any trade, profession or vocation" but extending beyond this narrow description to encompass "economic activity". The best determination of these ideas comes in the case authority which explores the limits of what is or is not a business for VAT purposes.[9]

Example: VAT chain

- Step 1: Hengist, a manufacturer, buys in material costing £20.00 and has overheads of £7.00 on which he incurs input tax of £3.50 and £1.20 respectively.

---

[7] Examples such as food, books, children's clothes are deemed socially essential and thus not to be penalised by being taxed.

[8] VATA 1994, s 4(1).

[9] *C & E Comrs* v *Lord Fisher* (1981); *C & E Comrs* v *Morrison's Academy Boarding Houses Association* (1978); *Three H Aircraft Hire* v *C & E Comrs* (1982).

- Step 2: Hengist sells to a wholesaler, Horsa, for £52.00. He charges output tax of £9.10, and deducts the input tax he has paid (totalling £4.70) and pays the balance of £4.40 to HMRC on his next VAT return.

- Step 3: Horsa in turn has overheads of £4.00 on which he has input tax of £0.70 but sells on to a retail shop, Maxico, for £65.00 and charges output tax of £11.40, deducts input tax he has paid (totalling £9.80) and pays the balance of £1.60 to HMRC in his next return.

- Step 4: Maxico sells to a consumer, Mr Public, for £100.00 on which the output tax is £17.50, and he deducts the input tax he has paid (£11.40) and pays the balance of £6.10 to HMRC.

The VAT fraction is the fraction used to work out the VAT quickly on a gross inclusive sale figure and is 7/47 on current UK standard-rated items. Where VAT is 17.5 per cent it is easy to see the VAT in a gross sale of £117.50 but more difficult where the gross figure is £6,000. The VAT fraction is applied to give the answer.

$$\frac{\text{VAT rate}}{100 + \text{VAT rate}} = \frac{7}{47} \qquad £6,000 \times \frac{7}{47} = £893.62$$

REVERSE CHARGE AND SELF-SUPPLY

In certain situations a UK taxable person must account for VAT as if the supply of goods or services concerned had been made to, and also by, himself. Output tax is accounted for to HMRC and the taxable person involved can recover the tax in the usual way as a claim on the VAT return for the period concerned. The most common situation where this happens is when there is a receipt of supplies from overseas countries outwith the EU. This legal fiction is known as the "reverse charge" or "self-supply" and is operated to ensure the continuation of the operation of the VAT commercial chain.[10] Another incidence is where a taxable person performs two tasks in the same commercial chain, such as a doctor who develops his own new surgical treatment complex and then operates this, once completed, as a provider of medical services; self-supply operates to prevent any illegal VAT advantage in the course of the development.

---

[10] VATA 1994, s 8.

GROUP REGISTRATION

Corporate bodies within common control can apply for a single or group registration for VAT purposes and this results in supplies of goods or services within the group which are not treated as chargeable transactions for VAT.[11] This is a sensible option for linked businesses and removes artificial "internal markets" within what are essentially the same entity and is also particularly attractive where members of a corporate group make exempt supplies and suffer restrictions on the recovery of input tax[12] but means that the registration is in the name of a representative member of the group which can be held accountable for the VAT returns of all members. The rules have been tightened and are strongly enforced to prevent any unfair advantage to corporations.[13]

Essential Facts

- VAT is a tax on transactions, which are the supply of goods or services made within a given jurisdiction by a taxable, non-exempt person.
- A person must be registered for VAT if the value of taxable supplies within the previous 12 months exceeds a certain limit.
- VAT is charged by the supplier and recovered by the customer at each stage of the commercial chain until the final consumer is reached who is not registered for VAT and thus pays the VAT cost.
- VAT covers all commercial transactions, though not all are subject to the standard VAT rate.

---

[11] VATA 1994, s 43.
[12] C & E Comrs v Kingfisher plc (1994).
[13] FA 2004 introduced a new s 43D to VATA 1994.

12 LOSSES AND CAPITAL ALLOWANCES

LOSSES

When an individual taxpayer or a partnership makes a loss there are two consequences:

(1) any tax assessment using that accounting period as its basis will have a nil assessment to tax;

(2) the loss may be utilised to reduce tax assessments of that or other years of assessment so that less tax will be paid or a claim for repayment of tax already paid will be entertained. Losses are personal to the taxpayer and cannot be bought or sold.

Types of loss relief

(1) *Income from property*: losses under the "income from property" provisions of ITTOIA 2005 (Sch A) are relievable only against similar types of profit.[1]

(2) *Trade and profession*: there are six main methods of relieving losses in trade and professional business under the Taxes Acts. All will require a formal request or election under the appropriate statutory measure and some are time limited:

- *carry forward* (ICTA 1988, s 385): the loss can be carried forward and set against the first available profits of the same business, without limit of time;

- *carry across or back* (ICTA 1988, s 380): the loss can be set against the total income of the taxpayer in the year in which the business loss arises. Alternatively, the loss can be carried back against taxpaying income from the preceding year;

- *early years* (ICTA 1988, s 381): a loss in the first year or the subsequent 3 years of a new business can be relieved under this measure, as an alternative to a claim under ss 380 or 385. The relief comes from set-off against the preceding 3 years' personal income prior to the loss;

- *final years* (ICTA 1988, s 386): where the business is transferred to a company in consideration for shares and the business has unrelieved losses, the proprietor can set-off the loss against

---

[1] There is an exception under ICTA 1988, s 379A for agricultural estates.

income he receives from the acquiring company in any subsequent year during which he still holds the shares, and as long as the company continues to trade;

- *terminal losses* (ICTA 1988, s 388): loss sustained in the last year of business that is not otherwise relieved under other measures, may be relieved against other business profits in the year of cessation and also against the preceding 3 years' profits;
- *capital gains* (FA 1991, s 72): trading losses can be set off against capital gains which arise in the year the loss arises and in 1 year preceding this. The relief is limited to the extent which the loss cannot be relieved against other statutory loss relief routes.

A number of loss relief exclusions were introduced by the anti-avoidance provisions in FA 2004 and FA 2005, which cover the manipulation of, among other things, partnership losses for non-active partners, and film investment losses on disposal of rights.

Companies

In contrast to the above business loss relief, company loss reliefs are available only to the company itself and never to the shareholders or directors as individuals. This can be a significant consideration when deciding whether to incorporate a business.

- *relief for trading losses: carry forward* (ICTA 1988, s 393): losses carry forward and are set against profits from the same trade in the future. Where there are insufficient trading profits, interest and dividends received can be used to offset the loss;
- *relief for trading losses against current and previous profits* (ICTA 1988, s 393A): losses are set against profits of the same or previous accounting periods; all profits and gains can be used.

Example: company loss

Hengist Ltd's accounts for the financial year show the following position:

	£
Letting income	11,000
Chargeable gains	9,000
	20,000
Less: Trading loss	(11,500)
Profits for corporation tax	£8,500

CAPITAL ALLOWANCES

The concept of an allowance for the reduction in the value of assets over time as a tax reducer was introduced in outline in Chapter 6. The legislation relating to capital allowances is contained in the Capital Allowances Act 2001 (CAA 2001) which came into effect for accounting periods ending on or after 1 April 2001 for corporation tax purposes and on 6 April 2001 for income tax purposes. Taxpayers cannot deduct capital expenditure in arriving at their taxable income or profits; neither is depreciation in commercial accounts allowed as a deduction for tax purposes. Capital allowances take the place of depreciation and allow the cost of most capital assets to be written down over time against the taxable profits of a business. Capital allowances match years of assessment to the accounting periods of a business and, where the accounting periods are not 12 months in duration, the capital allowances must be reduced or expanded to match. The capital allowance given each year is a fixed percentage of the value of the capital asset (or pool of assets, like a fleet of company cars) involved. The allowance is usually given on what is known as a *reducing balance basis*. The actual figure allowed in each year of assessment as a deduction from trading profit is known as the *writing down allowance* (WDA) and varies according to the type and lifespan of the asset involved (see below).

Rates

Main qualifying assets	First year/ initial allowance	Writing down allowance
Plant and machinery	40%*	25% (on tax WDV)
Industrial buildings	Abolished from 2011	4% (on cost)
Agricultural land and buildings	–	4% (on cost)
Hotels	–	4% (on cost)
Flat conversion	100%	25% (on cost)
Know-how	–	25% (on tax WDV)
Motor cars, other than low emission cars (max £3,000 allowance)	–	25% (on tax WDV)
Patent rights	–	25% (on tax WDV)
Research and development	100%	–

Special arrangements exist for the year in which a business ceases to trade, involving either a balancing charge or an allowance for assets sold off, depending on the price returned in comparison to the written down value (WDV). The legislation is not clear as to what precisely is included but is clearer on what is not included, so once again in UK tax matters we must look to the case law and judicial opinion.[2] What is clear is the distinction between capital and revenue expenditure which is central in ascertaining what may be claimed as a capital allowance, and this distinction is often difficult to draw.[3] Generally, assets that perform an active function in a business can safely be classed as eligible for capital allowances. Categories for capital allowances are as follows:

- *plant and machinery*: the apparatus used by a businessman for carrying on his business.[4] Thus it excludes trading stock and buildings and specifies that the assets must be actively used. The expenditure must be wholly and exclusively for the purpose of the trade and the capital items in the claim must belong to the business and cannot be leased;

- *industrial buildings*: these are defined in detail in the CAA 2001 as buildings or structures in use for the purpose of business, including mills, factories, mines or tunnels. Generally excluding domestic dwellings or retail shops, it can include a very wide variety of premises;

- *intellectual property*: CAA 2001, Pt 8: the ability to quantify and value intangible assets and to claim allowances for them; such as patents, copyrights and trademarks;

- *research and development*: FA 2000 and CAA 2001, Pt 6, ss 437–451: this covers creative or innovative work in the fields of science and technology;

- *agricultural assets*: defined under CAA 2001, Pt 4, as agricultural buildings and assets used in an agricultural business;

- *first year tax credits*: special incentives for "environmentally positive plant and machinery": added by FA 2008, s 79;

- *annual investment allowance* (AIA): applies to business of any size including traders and professionals. Claim AIA on any business-related capital expenditure up to £50,000.

---

[2] See Viscount Cave in *Atherton v British Insulated and Helsby Cables Ltd* (1926).
[3] *O'Grady v Bullcroft Main Collieries Ltd* (1932).
[4] *Yarmouth v France* (1887) and also *IRC v Barclay Curle & Co Ltd* (1969).

Capital allowances on a general pool for plant and machinery

	Pool £	Allowance £	£
Written down value b/f from previous year		200,000	
Additions in year		30,000	
		230,000	
Less: disposals in year		(35,000)	
		195,000	
WDA	(195,000 × 20%)	(39,000)	39,000
Written down value c/f to next year		156,000	

Essential Facts

- When a taxpayer makes a loss, any tax assessment using that accounting period as its basis will have a nil assessment to tax; and the loss may be utilised to reduce tax assessments of that or other years of assessment so that less tax will be paid.

- There are various types of loss relief, some of which require a formal request or election to be made within a certain time limit.

- Company loss reliefs are available only to the company itself and not to the shareholders or directors as individuals.

- Capital allowances are a fixed percentage of the value of the capital asset involved, usually on a reducing balance basis.

- The actual figure allowed in each year of assessment as a deduction from trading profit is known as the writing down allowance.

13 STAMP DUTY

There has been stamp duty in some form within at least part of what is now the United Kingdom[1] since 1694, with the modern variety being focused on two main areas:

(1) land and property conveyancing;

(2) transfers of UK company shares.

The distinguishing feature of stamp duty is that it is a charge on the execution of a legal instrument and not a charge on either a person or a transaction. Stamp taxes have particular relevance to legal and court practice as stamping is a requirement for many types of document to be formally registered and for use in evidence. The most recent modernisation of stamp tax in the UK was the introduction of stamp duty land tax (SDLT), by FA 2003, Pt 4 and which took effect from December 2003. Among other things, it paves the way for the introduction of electronic conveyancing. The new legislation abolished the old stamp duty regime except for transfers of stocks and securities. Stamp duty is calculated at either a flat rate or *ad valorem*, which means it varies according to the transaction to which it relates.

The rates of tax on transfers of property vary from 0 per cent to 4 per cent, depending on the property value, and the rates are not set up as cumulative bands in the way that income tax rates are, so that when a property price moves over a rate boundary the entire transaction is taxed at the higher rate band. The tax is always payable by the purchaser in a transaction to which it applies.

Transfers of land (consideration paid)

	Non-residential property	Residential property
0%	Up to £150,000	Up to £120,000
1%	£150,001–£250,000	£120,001–£250,000
3%	£250,001–£500,000	£250,001–£500,000
4%	Over £500,000	Over £500,000

There is a small increase in the threshold for the 0 per cent band where the property is in a disadvantaged area.

---

[1] I am grateful to my colleague Craig Anderson at Robert Gordon University for guidance on this point.

Example: SDLT

Andreas is bidding for two properties in good residential areas and will pay SDLT as follows:

- House 1: £244,000 in good area; therefore SDLT at 1% = £2,440;
- House 2: £255,000 in good area; therefore SDLT at 3% = £7,650.

The difference in rates of tax triggered by a small increase in price can be a significant factor in choice of property.

SDLT also applies to the grant of a lease and the net present value on the lease pays tax at the rates given below, with tax also due on any premium paid upon the granting of a new lease.

Grant of lease (net premium value of rent)

	Non-residential property	Residential property
0%	First £150,000	First £120,000
1%	Excess over £150,000	Excess over £120,000

Documents that need to be "stamped" should be submitted to one of the UK Stamp Duty offices, which are located in major towns and cities, within 30 days of the transaction occurring. This is subject to an interest and penalty regime, as with other UK tax enforcement policies. For SDLT on property, a self-assessment system is now in operation that requires the submission of a return by the purchaser within a 30-day period from the completion of the purchase or the lease agreement.

Essential Facts

- Stamp duty is a charge on the execution of a legal instrument and not a charge on either a person or a transaction.
- Stamp duty land tax was introduced by the Finance Act 2003, Pt 4, taking effect from December 2003.
- The old stamp duty regime has been abolished except for transfers of stocks and securities.
- Stamp duty is calculated at either a flat rate or *ad valorem* (varying according to the transaction to which it relates).

14 TAX PLANNING ISSUES AND ILLUSTRATIVE SCENARIOS

DISCLOSURE RULES

Professional advisers, including solicitors, accountants and financial advisers, are now required to disclose to HMRC all "notifiable proposals and arrangements",[1] which generally means arrangements under which a tax advantage is the main benefit to those using them. The Government advice makes it clear that the provisions do not apply to routine tax advice; however, the default position is that where tax advice is to be given, advance clearance should be sought from HMRC in order that the measures can be approved.[2]

The most recent updated version of the regulations came into effect on 1 July 2006. The regulations concern income tax, corporation tax and capital gains tax. Stamp duty land tax was brought within the disclosure regime with effect from 1 August 2005. The SDLT rules (found in the Stamp Duty Land Tax Avoidance Schemes (Prescribed Descriptions of Arrangements) Regulations (SI 2005/1868)) will continue to apply and are not affected by the latest proposals. It should also be noted that, following the coming into force of the national insurance contributions act 2006, a new s 132A of the Social Security Administration Act 1992 provides that any disclosure obligation relating to income tax can be extended by Treasury regulation to cover national insurance contributions and the disclosure rules apply to national insurance schemes with effect from 1 April 2007. Two draft statutory instruments have been published. The first seeks to amend reg 4 of the Information Regulations (SI 2004/1864) which deals with the due date for notifications. As the law currently stands, most notifications have to be made within 5 days after the "trigger" date.

In the case of notification of notifiable *proposals* by promoters, that trigger date is the earlier of:

- the date on which the promoter makes the proposal available for implementation by another person; and

---

[1] FA 2004, ss 306–319; and see Government advisory document "Disclosure of Direct Tax Avoidance Schemes" (July 2005).
[2] Tax Avoidance Schemes (Prescribed Descriptions of Arrangements) Regulations 2004 (SI 2004/1863).

- the date on which the promoter first becomes aware of any transaction forming part of notifiable arrangements implementing the notifiable proposal.

In the case of notification by promoters of notifiable *arrangements*, the trigger date is the date on which the promoter first becomes aware of any transaction forming part of any notifiable arrangements. Where there is a non-UK based promoter, it is the taxpayer who must notify HMRC within 5 days of the client first entering into a transaction forming part of the notifiable arrangements. Similarly, a 5-day notification period exists in respect of notifications by taxpayers where there is a promoter but the promoter's reporting obligations are subject to legal professional privilege.

TRUSTS FOR NON-DOMICILED INDIVIDUALS

For a non-domiciled individual, there are still significant tax advantages to creating an offshore trust. The exact advantages will depend upon the form of the settlement but, in general, the tax treatment is as follows:

- *income tax*: if the settlor is able to benefit from the settlement, then the income of the settlement will be treated as his own for income tax purposes, so the creation of the settlement will be income tax neutral. If the settlor is not able to benefit from the settlement, then the income tax treatment will vary according to the type of settlement;
- *CGT*: the trustees of the settlement can realise gains, on UK and non-UK assets alike, without being liable to pay CGT. However, realised gains are added to the settlement's "stockpiled gains", and these stockpiled gains are then attributed to beneficiaries who receive capital distributions from the settlement. However, non-UK domiciled beneficiaries are not liable to CGT on stockpiled gains, even if attributed to them. Thus, non-domiciled beneficiaries (including the settlor, if he is a beneficiary himself) can receive and remit capital distributions from an offshore settlement free of CGT;
- *IHT*: all non-UK located property in the settlement is excluded property and, as such, will be outside the scope of IHT;
- a non-UK domiciled settlor must take care before creating a settlement of UK-located property such as a house. Following the changes in Sch 20 to the Finance Act 2006, this will now be an immediately

chargeable transfer for IHT purposes, even if the settlement is on life interest trusts for the settlor himself, unless the assets being transferred are otherwise exempted, eg on the grounds of business property relief.

OPERATING THROUGH A PERSONAL SERVICE COMPANY (PSC)

Prior to IR35, a contractor was able to reduce the tax and national insurance contributions (NICs) lawfully due by setting off operating and administrative costs against revenue generated, by paying a salary to his spouse to take advantage of the lower rate tax bands and by paying some or all of the revenue generated through trading to himself or to family shareholders in the service company as dividends (which do not attract NICs).

The scope of IR35

IR35 is the reference number of the press release issue by the Inland Revenue on 9 March 1999 as part of the Chancellor's Budget statement for that year. The legislation came into force on 6 April 2000 and applies to a particular engagement where a contractor:

- alone or with any associates (family and unmarried partners), has a "material interest" in the service company, meaning ownership of more than 5 per cent of the issued ordinary share capital of the service company, an entitlement to more than 5 per cent of the dividends declared by the service company or (in the case of a closed company) to more than 5 per cent of the assets on the winding up of the service company
- receives a payment from the service company, which is not taxable under Sch E, that could reasonably be taken to represent payment for services provided by the contractor to a client of the service company, eg a dividend calculated on a quasi-commission basis in respect of fees generated by the contractor;

When IR35 applies

At the end of each tax year the service company must consider whether the IR35 legislation applies to any engagements undertaken by the contractor. If so, the service company must calculate whether all the fees generated from such IR35 engagements have been distributed to the contractor as salary or taxable benefits. The calculation permits the contractor to reduce the fees generated by a flat rate of 5 per cent in respect of administration costs. It also takes into account the employer's NICs paid by the service company, the expenses the contractor could claim if he were an employee and, to a limited extent, any additional travel expenses to and from the place of work. The outstanding balance of fees is referred to by the Inland Revenue as a "deemed payment" and is treated, for the purposes of calculating PAYE income tax and NICs, as if it had been paid to the contractor as salary during the relevant tax year. The service company therefore has a legal obligation to account for the income tax and the employer's and employee's NICs due on the deemed payment, regardless of whether any balancing payment is actually paid to the contractor.

The PCG's legal challenge

The Professional Contractors Group (PCG) applied to the High Court for a declaration that the IR35 legislation interfered with the "human right" of a service company peacefully to enjoy its possessions and that it was incompatible with European Union law because it was both an unlawful state aid to the larger corporate competitors of the service companies and an unlawful hindrance to free movement of workers, freedom of establishment and freedom to provide services. The application was dismissed on the following grounds:

- the High Court determined that the consequences of IR35 were not "even arguably so severe as to amount to a *de facto* confiscation of their property, to fundamental interference with their financial position or to an abuse of the United Kingdom's rights to levy taxes". This point was not pursued on appeal;
- the Court of Appeal agreed with the High Court's decision that the IR35 legislation is a general measure and stated that the aim of IR35 "is to ensure that individuals who ought to pay tax and NICs as employees cannot, by the assumption of a corporate structure, reduce and defer the liabilities imposed on employees by the United Kingdom's system of personal taxation". The court therefore determined that IR35 does not amount to unlawful state aid;
- the Court of Appeal held that "IR35 is not an obstacle to anyone who is seeking employment in the United Kingdom" and that Art 39, relating to the freedom of movement of workers, is not, therefore, applicable;

- the Court of Appeal held that IR35 was not discriminatory and "does not provide a direct and demonstrable inhibition on the establishment of a business within the United Kingdom, or on the provision of services without establishment".

Arctic Systems and post-IR35 arrangements

Jones v *Garnett (Inspector of Taxes)* (2007) illustrates the operation of the dangerous settlements code contained in ICTA 1988, s 660A (now transferred to ITTOIA 2005). Although defeated in the early stages, the taxpayer prevailed in the Court of Appeal and the House of Lords, and thus gives new hope for such "post-IR35 arrangements". The law, as it currently stands, is now very much in favour of the taxpayer. "Husband and wife" companies in which one spouse has a significant participation in the business but plays little role in the generation of business profits should be safe where the company's business is not involved in pre-ordained transactions or other arrangements which admit of an arrangement with unity of purpose and a very high degree of probability.

See also in this vein: *Cable & Wireless* v *Muscat* (2005) and also *Winter* v *Westward Television* (1977) and *Hewlett Packard* v *O'Murphy* (2002). These recent decisions have relevance for personal service companies and their clients. Where a client contracts with a service company, and that company provides the services of the worker to the client, established employment law has almost invariably held that the interposition of the company prevents the individual being employed by the client.

INCOME AND REMITTANCE PLANNING

Dual employment contracts

A UK-resident but non-UK-domiciled individual who performs a substantial part of his employment duties outside the UK may be able to divide his employment into two separate employments: one UK employment and one non-UK employment. The advantage of doing this is that employment income received from the non-UK employment is liable to UK income tax only on the remittance basis, so it can be paid offshore and kept outside the UK to fund foreign spending. The key to maintaining dual employment contracts is to be able to segregate different duties to be performed under each contract (and not merely the same duties in a different geographical location). For example, a fund manager could have duties of investment management while in the UK and duties of marketing while outside the UK. HMRC has taken a relaxed attitude to dual employment contracts, but its approach has changed and it now makes it clear that it will only accept dual contract arrangements where there are genuinely two positions that could be filled by two different people but which happen to be filled by the same person rather than one employment which has been artificially sub-divided.

Income and capital – split sources

This is the simplest method for mitigating a non-UK-domiciled person's income tax liability. If there is sufficient capital to fund his lifestyle in the UK, then he should maintain separate bank accounts for his capital and income. The capital account should be kept free of income or gains; interest accruing on the capital should automatically be paid into the income account, so that funds from the capital account can be remitted to the UK free of tax. The income account is instead used for non-UK spending. Other points to watch include foreign currency bank accounts and buying items outside the UK that are then brought into the UK (eg gifts, cars, etc), which will give rise to a remittance if the items are subsequently sold in the UK.

Cessation of source

Income is only taxable if it is from a taxable source: the "doctrine of source". A source cannot be taxable if it does not exist. Obviously, income cannot arise from a source that does not exist. However, income can arise from a source which, because of the deferral of charge under the remittance basis of taxation, does not exist at the time when the income is brought into charge.

Example

In April 2001, Rowan opens an offshore bank account. The account earns interest for 2 years, then Rowan closes it in April 2003. In April 2004, Rowan remits the earned interest. Since the source of the interest does not exist in the tax year during which it is brought into charge, it is outside the scope of income tax.

The application of this technique is now in practice limited to bank accounts and certain other investments. It does not apply to earned income, which is deemed by statute to be income from the last year of employment, whenever remitted. Nor does it apply to capital gains. Also, this is rarely useful where the income is distributed by a discretionary settlement, since the settlement will generally be the source of the income.

Loans

Some non-UK income can effectively be enjoyed in the UK, without constituting a remittance, if the non-UK-domiciled taxpayer takes out a loan offshore, brings the loan proceeds into the UK for UK spending, and pays the loan interest out of non-UK income. It is essential here that the loan is taken out offshore and the proceeds subsequently brought into the UK; the tax treatment is different if the loan is taken out in the UK from an offshore lender. Any repayment of loan principal out of non-UK income of capital gains would constitute a remittance.

Completed gifts

A completed gift can be a very effective way of "cleaning out" non-UK income which would otherwise be taxed on the remittance basis, provided that the non-UK-domiciled taxpayer intends to make a real gift, and there are no arrangements under which he receives a corresponding benefit. The gift, in the hands of the recipient, is "clean" capital. The recipient will not be subject to income tax on receiving the gift, even if UK domiciled, and can bring the gift proceeds into the UK without giving rise to a chargeable remittance but should do so in a subsequent tax year. However, it is essential that the gift should be completed outside the UK, otherwise there may be a remittance by the donor. It is also essential that the donor should not receive some benefit out of the gift proceeds, nor any corresponding benefit from the recipient, otherwise HMRC may consider the gift to be merely a conduit through which the donor has made a remittance to the UK. There is Court of Appeal authority in *Grimm v Newman* (2002) for the proposition that "an expectation as to the use [the recipient] might put the gift" is not sufficient to create a conduit. However, this will not assist the taxpayer where the benefit to the donor is pre-ordained at the time of the gift.

PROBLEM SCENARIOS

Scenario A

O'Neill sells his factory in November 2006 for £250,000 and opts to site his business in rented premises in order to release cash flow. The factory had been purchased in April 1984 (RPI 88.64) for £100,000. O'Neill had purchased fixed operating plant in December 2003, costing £240,000, and has elected to "hold over" any gain on the factory against the cost of the plant.

You are asked to:

1. calculate the chargeable gain on the sale of the factory (before any taper relief) and the effect of the "hold over" claim on that gain. (RPI April 1998: 162.6);
2. advise on the earliest time at which the "hold over" would cease to be effective.

Scenario B

Mr Larsson is a Swedish citizen. He owns a house in Helsingborg and regards Sweden as his home but lives in Glasgow for nearly all of tax year 2008–09. His income for the year is from the following sources:

1. part-time employment with a Glasgow company (duties performed there);
2. part-time employment with a Swedish company (duties performed there on his monthly visits);
3. dividends from stocks and shares held in Sweden;
4. interest on UK Government stocks.

To what extent is he liable to UK income tax on these situations?

Scenario C

In August 1999 Isolde gave £500,000 to her daughter as a wedding present. In June 2003 she gave a further £500,000 to a discretionary trust. Isolde died amid the New Year celebrations in Stonehaven on 1 January 2005, having made only these two transfers in her life.

1. Calculate the tax due on these transfers at the time of their making. When is the tax due for payment, assuming that it is paid by the donor?
2. Calculate the tax due upon death and the date of payment by executors.

Scenario D

Athen-Rye Ltd makes up accounts to 31 March each year. In the period to 31 March 2005 results are as follows:

	£	£
Trading profit	170,000	
Capital allowances		32,000
Rental income	46,000	
Capital gains	6,400	

The company has capital losses brought forward from previous accounting periods of £1,400 and made gift aid donation to disaster relief of £20,000 at the end of the trading year. The company also received a dividend from Freebird plc in December 2004 of £14,400.

1. Calculate the corporation tax due for the year to 31 March 2005.

2. If all 1,000 shares in Athen-Rye are held equally by its founders (Messrs O'Neill and Craig), suggest how they might simply reduce this liability for the year in question.

SOLUTIONS TO SCENARIOS

Scenario A

1. Gain on disposal of building is:

		£
Sale proceeds		250,000
Less: Acquisition cost	100,000	
		150,000
Less: Indexation allowance		
$\dfrac{162.6 - 88.64}{88.64}$	= 0.834 × £100,000	
		83,400
		66,600
Less: "Held over" gain	56,600	
Net chargeable gain		10,000

2. The "held over" gain is deferred until the earliest of:

- disposal of the plant;
- December 2013 (10 years after acquisition);
- the date it ceases to be used in the business.

Scenario B

Larsson is a UK resident for 2008–09 but he is neither ordinarily resident nor domiciled in the UK. His UK tax position is therefore as follows:

- earnings from UK employment are fully taxable;
- earnings from Swedish employment are taxable but only on a remittance basis. This would be the case even if he were tax resident in the UK ("foreign earnings" rule);
- dividends are assessed under Sch D, Case V, on a remittance basis;

- interest on UK Government stocks is exempt from UK income tax as Larsson is not ordinarily resident in the UK;
- he is able to claim personal allowances for 2008–09.

Scenario C

The value of each gift after deduction of exemptions is as follows:

	Value before AE £	AE for current year £	AE for previous year £	Value after AE £
1999–2000 Daughter (£500,000–£5,000)	495,000	3,000	3,000	489,000
2003–04 Discretionary trust	500,000	3,000	3,000	494,000

Lifetime tax liability

The gift to Isolde's daughter was a PET, so no lifetime tax was payable. The lifetime tax on the gift to the discretionary trust was £59,750, payable on 30 April 2004 and calculated as follows:

	Net £	Gross £	Tax £
£255,000 grossed up @ 0%	255,000	255,000	0
£239,000 grossed up @ 20%	239,000	298,750	59,750
	494,000	553,750	59,750

Tax liability on death

(i) *Transfer made on 31 August 1999*

The gross value of this transfer is £489,000 and there were no chargeable transfers in the 7 years ending on the date of the transfer. Tax due at death rates applicable on 1 January 2005:

	£
£263,000 @ 0%	0
£226,000 @ 40%	90,400
	90,400
Less: Taper relief (5–6 years) @ 60%	54,240
	36,160
Less: Lifetime tax paid	0
IHT payable by daughter on 31 July 2005	36,160

(ii) Transfer made on 1 June 2003

The gross value of this transfer is £553,750 and previous gross chargeable transfers in the 7 years ending on the date of the transfer (2 June 1996 to 1 June 2003) were £489,000, which used the whole of the 0% band. Tax due at death rates applicable on 1 January 2005:

	£
553,750 @ 40%	221,500
Less: Taper relief (0–3 years) @ 0%	0
	221,500
Less: Lifetime tax paid	59,750
IHT payable by trustees on 31 July 2005	161,750

Scenario D

1.

	£
Trading profits	170,000
Less: Capital allowances	32,000
Sch D (now under CTA 2009)	138,000
Lettings	46,000
Capital gains £6,400–£1,400	5,000
	189,000
Less: Charges on income	20,000
Chargeable profits	169,000
FII (£14,400 + £1,600)	16,000
Profits	185,000
Corporation tax at 20%, due 1 January 2009	37,000

2. Use the dividend route. This varies the tax rate and postpones payment of the tax due until January 2010.

Essential Facts

- Disclosure rules now require all professional advisers to disclose to HMRC all "notifiable proposals and arrangements", which generally means arrangements under which a tax advantage is the main benefit to those using them.
- For a non-domiciled individual, there are still significant tax advantages to creating an offshore trust.
- IR35 legislation applies to certain engagements undertaken by contractors.
- Dual employment contracts have the advantage that employment income received from the non-UK employment is liable to UK income tax only on the remittance basis, so it can be paid offshore and kept outside the UK to fund foreign spending.
- A non-UK-domiciled person's income tax liability can be mitigated by his maintaining separate bank accounts for his capital and income.

15 AN AGE OF CHANGE: NEW COURTS FOR THE UK

THE NEW TAX TRIBUNAL

Since the merger of the Inland Revenue and HM Customs & Excise in 2005, one of the main projects for HM Treasury has been modernising the way in which compliance is handled. Compliance, in simple terms, is the collective term for the methods used to ensure taxpaying entities in all legal forms are doing what they are required to do by the law and for the adjudication of disputes that result when they, apparently, are not.

This process inevitably involves a certain amount of intervention by the tax authorities, now unified as HMRC. With the advent of the new dedicated tax tribunal system, already referred to in professional circles as the "tax chamber", this chapter considers whether the above requirements have been met.

TAX CHAMBER: TRIBUNAL

The creation of the new tax chamber has been facilitated by the Tribunals, Courts and Enforcement Act 2007 (TCEA 2007).[1] The Act creates a two-tier structure with a first-tier and upper tribunal system, and with individual tribunal jurisdictions doing similar work being brought together into a simplified two-tier system. The new system, headed by Lord Justice Carnwath as senior president, is designed to improve service delivery and bring together the expertise that exists in each tribunal jurisdiction.

Since 2005, HMRC has been responsible for enforcing and administering the payment of both direct and indirect taxes. In this context, it is arguably inconsistent to maintain four separate tax tribunals (the General Commissioners, the Special Commissioners, the VAT and Duties Tribunal and the Section 702/706 Tribunal) and the three different sets of legal rules required for those tribunals.

These factors, together with increasing pressure from the EU Commission and the European Court of Justice and a succession of Government reports recommending reform, most notably that of Sir Andrew Leggatt, *Tribunals for users – one system, one service* in 2001, indicated that the time had arrived for the creation of a unified tax chamber. This

---

[1] TCEA 2007: relevant measures regarding the tax tribunals came into force on 1 April 2009.

process may in turn eventually lead to a specialist tax court for the UK as currently seen in many jurisdictions.

The new system which came into force in April 2009 has its own specialist judiciary, rules of procedure and a new location for processing direct tax appeals. It is independent of HMRC, which previously controlled listing and other aspects of case management in the old system. In fact, the old system was often seen as not sufficiently distanced from the department; the old Latin maxim *nemo iudex in causa sua* (ie no one should be the judge in their own case), comes to mind.

THE JUDICIARY AND ITS RULES

All parties concerned in tax compliance welcomed the advent of a professional and independently appointed judiciary to deal with tax appeals in the UK as a significant step towards consistency and legal certainty in the regulation of disputes.

In partnership with the Judicial Appointments Commission, the Government has recruited 18 legal members, four of whom will be full time, and 75 non-legal member positions. The new posts were filled and the training process completed in time for the launch of the system in April 2009 and the first year of operation has gone without obvious or major difficulty, certainly up to the time of writing.[2]

The legislation establishes the Tribunals Procedure Committee (TPC) which makes and amends rules governing the practice and procedure in the tribunals, including those of the tax chamber. The First-tier Tax Chamber Rules were agreed by the committee subject to consultation, which ran for the 6 months from its announcement in August 2008 until January of 2009.

THE CONSULTATION

The consultation sought views on the new system and its procedures in their entirety as well as on any individual rules, with the aim of achieving a system which is both flexible and practical but also appropriate to the range of matters heard in the tax jurisdiction.

In due credit to this process, many of the views gathered were given due weight in the run-up to full implementation in April 2009.

The Ministry of Justice set up the consultations under two specific headings:

---

[2] The first year of operation is complete at time of writing (June 2010).

- first, on the rules for the first-tier tribunal, the tax chamber, where most tax cases will start, and included draft rules for comment. These were approved after significant input from the consultation process;
- second, there was a request for suggestions as to how the rules for the upper tribunal, which will hear appeals from the first-tier tribunal, should be adapted for tax cases.

The crucially important matter of costs in the upper tribunal and any system of alleviating them to ensure a degree of equal access to the process still remains unresolved and not subject to formal ongoing consultation as the now established rules contain only a very limited provision in this regard. However, the Ministry of Justice has indicated that it would consider costs orders for tax appeals on a case-by-case basis.

As currently practised in the new system, unless an appeal is allocated to the "complex" track, costs in the first-tier tribunal and the upper tribunal will be treated in a manner similar to that previously applied to the Special Commissioners under the old system. Given that the new system will be uniform for all types of tax appeals, this amounts to a significant restriction for taxpayers when compared to the current position for appeals to the VAT and Duties Tribunal and to the High Court or Court of Exchequer in Scotland.

This restriction in the ability for taxpayers to recover costs in the upper tribunal is likely to discourage taxpayers with potentially robust cases from appealing; and this, in turn, raises concerns over access to justice and about inequality of arms. However, this last issue was acknowledged by the ministry in the consultation papers and can currently be described as "work in progress" for the new regime.

TAXPAYERS' ADVOCATE SERVICE

In seeking best practice solutions for important issues, perhaps the UK should look to the experience of the United States and the Internal Revenue Service (IRS) and consider setting up a taxpayers' advocate service.[3]

In the US, this is an independent organisation, which is supported and promoted by the IRS. It also works with the IRS in resolving tax issues outwith the formality of the court system.

---

[3] See R Maas, "A Helping Hand", *Taxation* (September 2007).

The American view is that there is much to be gained from having advocates who know the system and yet are genuinely independent, and can also report independently to the formal judicial process.

In its "Taxpayer bill of rights", the US Congress not only established the Office of the Taxpayer Advocate but also described its functions:

- to assist taxpayers in resolving problems with the IRS;
- to identify areas in which taxpayers have problems in dealings with the IRS;
- to the extent possible, to propose changes in the administrative practices of the IRS to mitigate those identified problems; and
- to identify potential legislative changes which may be appropriate to mitigate such problems.

This seems to represent a fairly well-defined service which seeks to perform in the public interest, guaranteed in law. It will be interesting to see, in the coming months and years, the extent to which the new UK system lives up to these goals.

THE NEW AGE

Under the new UK system, the main differences we see from the old Taxes Management Act procedure is that appeal notices are sent directly to the Tribunals Service by the appellant, rather than to HMRC, and there are four procedural tracks depending on the complexity of the appeal.

Members of the judicial team work at the Central Processing Centre in Birmingham, which has an effective headquarters function, in order to give legal direction where required and manage cases appropriately. There are also two full-time, tax-dedicated registrars at the centre, who carry out quasi-judicial functions, such as:

- categorisation of cases received at the centre into tracks, as laid down in the proposed rules of procedure;
- identification of tax cases which are complex, and bringing these to the attention of the judiciary for a decision;
- liaison with the upper tribunal regarding those rare cases which start at that court, or which appeal to it from the first-tier.

The route of appeal from the first-tier will be to the upper tribunal, which is a superior court of record similar to the High Court. Appeal to the upper tribunal is on a point of law only, and with permission of the first-tier or the upper tribunal. The exceptions to this are those rare cases which start in the upper tribunal, where onward appeals will be to the Court of Appeal or the Court of Exchequer in Scotland.

INTERNAL REVIEW

Sir Andrew Leggatt, in his original report, recommended sweeping changes to the tribunal system. However, he also recommended that government should consider the scope for internal review of decisions and procedures within HMRC.

The real issue for HMRC is how to achieve a review system that is impartial, cost effective, and will not duplicate the work of the new tribunal system itself. The current interim working solution, which seems highly cost sensitive, is to keep the process in-house. The problem is then how to ensure that such a review is actually impartial, though it must be said there have been no such specific complaints so far.

The idea is that the review be conducted by someone other than the immediate line manager, who is not involved in the original decision. The fundamental question for disgruntled taxpayers and agents is what should be done to ensure that such a review is indeed impartial.

It goes almost without saying that the problem for any reviewer is that he may need to go back to the case officer for further information and this contact alone could create bias.

The consultation also asked whether a review should be statutory or non-statutory, and whether there should be uniformity of approach across the different taxes. These are important questions.

One of the points of this reform process is, given that the previous system is non-statutory and inconsistent, it is designed fundamentally to replace such disparate systems (which have developed for historical reasons) with a single tax appeals system. HMRC's view is apparently that one review procedure may not be suitable for all types of tax, thus allowing for different procedures on different types of tax, but additionally it suggests that a common time limit for review might be simpler and more cost effective.

REFORMS PROJECT

HMRC is continuing to run a tribunals' reform project addressing the impact of the launch of the tax chamber, seeking feedback from professionals and taxpayers on the operation of the new system and the internal review process, as part of the settling-in process.

The enabling instrument, the Transfer of Tribunal Functions, Revenue and Customs Order 2008, passed into law on 26 November of that year. The order has two main purposes: the first is to transfer tax tribunal functions and existing judiciary into the new tribunals established under TCEA 2007; the second is to set out new processes for HMRC handling of disputes prior to their reaching the tribunal. The passing of the order will enable tax tribunal reform and also enable changes to the way HMRC handles appeals prior to their reaching the new, unified tax jurisdiction.

It is to be hoped that, despite all the changes, the UK can retain the best features of the former system of tax administration and appeals in the new system. It will retain access to local hearings through the network of centres across the country and in the recruitment of the new judiciary from a wide geographical area. Local business knowledge will be retained as an important feature, together with an element of social diversity.

The changes are long overdue and herald a great opportunity for what Adam Smith set out over two centuries ago: a tax system with certainty, efficiency and fairness at its core. From the few cases to have graced the new procedure so far, the system seems to operate to the satisfaction of all parties to the disputes,[4] with *Colquhoun* (2010) being a reasonable test of the system being a classic avoidance theory case. We will, however, have to wait and see as it is still early days to make a compelling verdict on the new arrangements.

THE UK SUPREME COURT

Another major change to the UK courts system which has general impact on the administration of law and the courts, and has specific impact on the adjudication and administration of tax cases above the level discussed in the preceding paragraphs, is the advent of the new Supreme Court. The Supreme Court of the United Kingdom is the court of last resort, the highest appellate court in all matters under English law, Welsh law, Northern Irish law and Scottish civil law, though the Court has no authority over criminal cases in Scotland, where the High Court of Justiciary remains the supreme criminal court. The Supreme Court also has jurisdiction to determine devolution disputes – cases in which the legal powers of the three devolved Governments, or laws made by the devolved legislatures, are questioned.

---

[4] See *Colqhuoun* v *HMRC* (2010) (United Kingdom First-tier Tribunal).

The Supreme Court sits in the Middlesex Guildhall in Westminster, London, which it shares with the Judicial Committee of the Privy Council.

The Supreme Court was established by Pt 3 of the Constitutional Reform Act 2005 and started work on 1 October 2009. It assumed the judicial functions of the House of Lords, which were exercised by the Lords of Appeal in Ordinary (commonly called "Law Lords"), the 12 professional judges appointed as members of the House of Lords to carry out its judicial business. Its jurisdiction over devolution matters had previously been held by the Judicial Committee of the Privy Council.

The main role of the UK Supreme Court is to hear appeals from courts in the United Kingdom's three legal systems: England and Wales, Northern Ireland, and Scotland. (English and Welsh law differ only to the extent that the National Assembly for Wales makes laws for Wales that differ from those in England.) The Supreme Court acts as the highest court for civil appeals from the Court of Session in Scotland but the highest appeal for criminal cases is kept in Scotland. It may hear appeals from the civil Court of Session, just as the House of Lords did previously.

From the Court of Session, permission to appeal is not required and any case can proceed to the Supreme Court of the United Kingdom if two Advocates certify that an appeal is suitable. In England, Wales and Northern Ireland, leave to appeal is required either from the Court of Appeal or from a Justice of the Supreme Court itself.

The Court's focus is on cases that raise points of law of general public importance. Like the previous Appellate Committee of the House of Lords, appeals from many fields of law are likely to be selected for hearing – including commercial disputes, family matters, judicial review claims against public authorities and issues under the Human Rights Act 1998. The Court also hears some criminal appeals, but not from Scotland as there is no right of appeal from the High Court of Justiciary, Scotland's highest criminal court.

The Supreme Court also determines "devolution issues" (as defined by the Scotland Act 1998, the Northern Ireland Act 1998 and the Government of Wales Act 2006). These are legal proceedings about the powers of the three devolved administrations: the Northern Ireland Executive and Northern Ireland Assembly, the Scottish Government and the Scottish Parliament, and the Welsh Assembly Government and the National Assembly for Wales. Devolution issues were previously heard by the Judicial Committee of the Privy Council and most are about compliance with rights under the European Convention on Human

Rights, brought into national law by the devolution Acts and the Human Rights Act 1998.

In the exercise of this jurisdiction, the Supreme Court's supremacy is affirmed by s 41(3), which states that a decision of the Court on a devolution matter is binding in all legal proceedings.

The Supreme Court has come into being at a time when the United Kingdom's devolution jurisprudence is conspicuous by its relative absence; and questions about the scope of powers devolved to Scotland, Northern Ireland and Wales will undoubtedly arise, notwithstanding the availability of legislative consents known as "Sewel" motions. It is also possible that the fulfilment of the Court's duty to determine the validity of statutes in its devolution jurisdiction might influence its desire and approach to reviewing statutes in other spheres such as under the Human Rights Act 1998, s 3, even though the relevant remedy is a declaration of incompatibility, rather than invalidity, and vice versa.

The establishment of the Supreme Court of the United Kingdom represents a significant constitutional reform, one which is long overdue. Its arrival was somewhat overshadowed by real concerns as to the manner of the Court's creation, which seemed to many to be rushed and lacking attention to detail over the finer points of its role. However, independence and a true separation of powers is no mere formality and even the enhanced perception of judicial independence is to be welcomed.

16 COALITION GOVERNMENT EMERGENCY BUDGET: 22 JUNE 2010

The Budget of the coalition Government elected on 6 May 2010 lived up to expectations of being tough, with everyone having to pay something towards reducing the UK national deficit. Certainly, there wasn't much to celebrate in the content, which made for grim reading in all departments and will make for further complexity in the Finance Act 2010 when it is finalised.

PERSONAL TAX

As had been indicated, the Chancellor announced that the usual increase in the personal tax allowance for 2011/12 will be overridden and increased by £1,000 to £7,475 for those aged under 65. This will reduce tax bills by up to £200 for basic-rate taxpayers. Higher-rate taxpayers will not benefit because the basic-rate limit will be reduced by a figure to be confirmed once the September RPI figure is known.

NATIONAL INSURANCE

While the previously planned increase in National Insurance contributions will go ahead with effect from 6 April 2011, the secondary threshold, the point at which employers start to pay Class 1 NICs, will be increased by an extra £21 per week above indexation.

In another measure designed to encourage new businesses and new employments, the Budget speech included an announcement that anyone setting up a new business outside of London, the south-east and the eastern region will be exempt from up to £5,000 of employer NICs for each of the first 10 employees hired. The scheme will be operational from September 2010, but will apply from Budget Day, 22 June 2010. To maintain the alignment of the upper earnings/profits limit with the higher-rate tax threshold, the UEL/UPL will be reduced by an equivalent amount.

CAPITAL GAINS TAX

It was feared that capital gains tax rates would be raised to the level of income tax rates, but the rates applicable from Budget Day are to be 18 per cent and 28 per cent. So, no change for basic-rate taxpayers but, from

Budget Day, taxpayers on higher rates will pay 28 per cent on their capital gains.

Perhaps unsurprisingly, closer investigation of Budget Note BN20 shows that "the rate of CGT remains 18% where total taxable gains and income are less than the upper limit of the income tax basic rate band. The 28% rate applies to gains above that limit".

On the subject of CGT: for trustees and personal representatives, the rate is increased from 18 per cent to 28 per cent; the annual exempt amount will remain at £10,100 for 2010/11 (but is planned to rise with inflation in future); and the 10 per cent rate for entrepreneurs' relief remains, but with the lifetime relief limit raised from £2 million to £5 million.

BN20 also explains that gains arising between 6 April and 22 June 2010 – and chargeable at 18 per cent – will not be taken into account in determining the rate of tax applicable to gains arising after that period.

However, pre-23 June 2010, gains that are deferred until after that date will be chargeable at 18 per cent or 28 per cent in the same way as any other gain arising after 23 June 2010.

Regarding losses and the annual exemption for 2010/11, it is stated that these can be used in the manner most beneficial to the taxpayer.

Things could have been a lot harsher for those facing CGT bills this year. Indeed, some taxpayers may even be celebrating a reduced tax bill from an increase in the limit of entrepreneurs' relief.

Individuals who qualify for the lower 10 per cent rate of capital gains tax on the disposal of certain business assets (by virtue of entrepreneurs' relief) will be pleased to see that the extent of that relief has been extended. Entrepreneurs' relief applies so that an effective 10 per cent rate of CGT is available on the disposal of qualifying holdings in trading companies, where the shareholder is an employee or director of the company. Prior to the Budget Day announcement, the 10 per cent rate was restricted to a lifetime limit of £2 million of capital gains. However, for disposals taking place from 23 June 2010 onwards, this limit has been increased to £5 million. The mechanism for providing such relief has also been altered to allow for the differing rates of capital gains tax.

The date of disposal for CGT purposes occurs on the date of an unconditional agreement to sell, assuming that the agreement is completed in due course. Therefore those who have already entered into unconditional agreements to dispose of capital assets will remain subject to the old regime.

PENSIONS

Better news in relation to pensions in the Budget. First, there could be some relief for the much-reviled measures restricting higher-rate relief on pension contributions.

While the Chancellor believes that reform is "necessary", he has apparently "listened to the concerns of the pensions industry and employers", and realised that "the approach adopted in Finance Act 2010 ... could have unwelcome consequences for pension saving, bring significant complexity to the tax system, and damage UK business and competitiveness".

It seems that the Government is considering the alternative approach involving a reduced annual allowance, as was mooted by many in the pensions industry, including the National Association of Pension Funds, before the March Budget. To this end, the Government will consult employers, pension schemes, experts and other interested parties to determine the best design of a regime. The idea is to introduce legislation before the summer recess, to repeal, through regulations, the legislation passed at the Finance Act 2010 once it has decided on the detail of its approach. There will, however, be no changes to the anti-forestalling regime.

The Chancellor plans to end, from April 2011, the existing rules that create an effective obligation to purchase an annuity by age 75. Legislation will be introduced in the Finance Bill 2010 to increase the age to 77. The change will apply for the purposes of the inheritance tax charges that specifically apply to pension scheme members aged 75 and over.

With regard to the state pension, this is to be realigned to the earnings index when it comes to annual increases. In future it will be uprated by either earnings, prices or 2.5 per cent, whichever is the higher.

Finally, the Chancellor announced that the move to a state pension age of 66 is to be accelerated, and he also said there would be a consultation on the removal of the default retirement age: the ability of employers to force workers to retire at age 65.

BUSINESS TAX

On the basis that "low rates act as corporate magnets for the countries that introduce them" the rate of mainstream corporation tax has been reduced to 27 per cent from 1 April 2011, and then further reduced by 1 per cent for each of the following years until it settles at 24 per cent in April 2014. This gives the UK one of the lowest rates in the G20 and the lowest rate the UK has ever known.

Those dealing with the oil industry should note that the rate for profits from oil extraction and rights remains at 30 per cent.

Rumours had been circulating that if mainstream rates were reduced, then the small companies rate might be abolished. However, in something of a surprise move, it was announced that, rather than increasing this to 22 per cent as planned by the previous Government, the rate was to be cut to 20 per cent with effect from 1 April 2011. This was estimated to help 850,000 companies, who would also be assisted by an extension of the Enterprise Finance Guarantee scheme. The equivalent rate for the oil industry will be 19 per cent.

Presumably to help pay for the reduction in CT taxes, the rates of capital allowances are to be lowered. The rate for most plant and machinery falls from 20 per cent to 18 per cent, and for long-life assets from 10 per cent to 8 per cent. The annual investment allowance is reduced to £25,000; all measures are effective from April 2012.

The Government no doubt hopes that the rate reductions will stem the flow of companies relocating abroad, although some firms may find their effective rate of tax increases due to the reduction in the rates of capital allowances and the reduced annual investment allowance.

Conversely, proprietors of smaller businesses may consider the advantages of incorporation to shelter profits at the reduced 20 per cent rate.

There were winners and losers in specific industries. The advantageous tax rules for furnished holiday lettings (FHLs) are to be retained, but the planned relief for the video games industry is scrapped.

With regard to FHLs, there is certainty, for a year at least, in that the Chancellor is reinstating the previous tax rules, which were to have been abolished. However, the Government plans to consult over the summer on a proposal to ensure that the tax rules meet EU legal requirements by changing the eligibility thresholds and restricting loss reliefs. Changes will take effect from April 2011.

In addition to the main changes discussed above, the Budget documents include a paragraph to the effect that the Government is committed to reviewing IR35 and small business tax. This is welcome news, and the further details promised are anticipated eagerly.

Further measures of interest to business announced in the Budget report are consultations on: a reform of the controlled foreign company rules; a move to a more territorial basis for taxing the profits of foreign branches; the taxation of intellectual property, research and development tax credits; and the proposals of the Dyson Review.

VAT

In another measure that had been widely anticipated, the standard rate of VAT was increased to 20 per cent from 4 January 2011, the first working day of the new year.

The procedures, for example, for anti-forestalling legislation, are similar from when the rate went from 15 per cent to 17.5 per cent at the beginning of 2010. The threshold is again £100,000 and will not be an issue if a customer can claim input tax or if a transaction is usual commercial practice, for example, a quarterly rental invoice raised in advance.

The other main issues with the rate change are as follows:

- it is worthwhile for businesses to buy their new motor cars before 4 January 2011, because the input tax block that applies on motor cars will mean an extra cost with the rate change;

- commercial property bought by exempt or partly exempt businesses should ideally be completed before the January date, otherwise a further cost will be relevant through the input tax restrictions for these businesses;

- there is concern about the impact of the rate increases on charities and other organisations where they have received grant offers based on a 17.5 per cent VAT cost but where the project will be carried out in 2011. Perhaps grant providers might offer a bit of flexibility with an additional grant to cover the VAT increase?

On the positive side, there are plenty of items where VAT is not charged because of zero-rating and exemption.

UK BANK LEVY

Still blamed by most for sparking off the worst recession in decades, bankers did not come off unscathed in the Budget. The Chancellor announced that there will be a bank levy, based on balance sheet liabilities, to be introduced from 1 January 2011. In a joint statement with France and Germany, the levy is aimed at encouraging banks "to move to less risky funding profiles". The levy will not be deductible for corporation tax, and there will be anti-avoidance provisions.

This will affect all UK banks and banking groups as well as non-UK banking groups with UK operations, although only in both cases if they have relevant liabilities of £20 billion or more. Tier 1 capital, insured retail deposits, repos secured on sovereign debt and policyholder liabilities of retail insurance businesses within banking groups will not be included as liabilities for this purpose. It is also proposed that only net derivative liabilities will be included.

Unlike bank payroll tax, the proposed bank levy is to be a permanent levy, although it will also not be corporation tax deductible. The rate is proposed to be set at 0.04 per cent in 2011, rising to 0.07 per cent in later years. There will be a reduced rate for longer-maturity wholesale funding liabilities of 0.02 per cent and 0.035 per cent respectively. Staff remuneration and bank profitability play no part in calculating the levy (although there are separate Government initiatives looking at taxes linked to these), but the final scope of the levy will no doubt be subject to international G20 developments where taxing financial transactions and other activities are still being discussed. The UK Government will not legislate in a vacuum, although a Government press release issued at the time of the Budget said that the French and German Governments are also pursuing a balance sheet-based levy.

There will be consultation in advance of the levy coming into effect in January 2011. It is hoped that the levy's scope will be clear from the outset, unlike the bank payroll tax where there had to be a significant battle to make the tax appropriately targeted. However, there will be key things to consider, such as when the measurement date for liabilities is to be and whether it is only amounts above £20 billion that will be taxed or whether, if a bank is caught, all relevant liabilities will be subject to the levy. It is also not clear whether the liabilities of a an overseas branch of a bank will be subject to double taxation, ie taxed in two countries' banking tax systems, or whether there would somehow be the ability to credit one payment against the other liability. Finally, close scrutiny will need to be paid as to whether just banking liabilities are caught or liabilities relating to non-banking activities also are included.

THE REDUCTIONS IN CORPORATION TAX BALANCED BY LOWER CAPITAL ALLOWANCES

The planned changes to capital allowances were certainly less bad than had been anticipated. There were proposals from the Conservatives in Opposition that there would be a massive "cut" of capital allowances to pave the way for the reduction in corporation tax rates.

In the event, the Chancellor has taken a more balanced approach by phasing in the reduction in corporation tax rates, and at the same time taking a less aggressive attitude to the cuts in capital allowances.

REDUCTION IN ANNUAL INVESTMENT ALLOWANCE

When the annual investment allowance was introduced in 2008, the then Chancellor announced that 98 per cent of all businesses would have their capital spend covered in full by the new allowance – set at an annual limit of £50,000.

In 2010, in a throwaway measure, the limit for a year was increased to £100,000. This increase was hardly of benefit to smaller businesses – by definition – apart from those who have an occasional need to spend large sums of money. So the change which comes in from April 2012 covers all of the bases. It reduces the annual limit to £25,000 from the current level of £100,000, allowing businesses which need to make one-off large spends the time to put finances in place to make the purchase in 2010. It also retains the benefit of simplification for smaller businesses which do not need to compute allowances for tax purposes, and will generally see their equipment allowed for tax as they incur the expenditure.

CHANGES IN RATES

A small reduction in the rates of capital allowances for both the main pool and the special rate pool will save quite significant sums of money – that is, costs are measured on a cash basis and not on an accruals basis. It is true that all businesses will still get the benefit of tax relief on the equipment that they purchase, but they will receive this tax benefit at a slightly slower rate than they would otherwise do. Another neat trick is to reduce the rate of writing down allowance from April 2012, while the reduction in the main rate of corporation tax is phased in over 4 years.

Overall, the impact of the reduction as compared with both the current and recent rates of WDA is as follows:

Rate of WDA %	Time to write off 80% (years)	Time to write off 90% (years)	Time to write off 95% (years)
6	27	38	49
8	20	28	36
10	16	22	29
18	9	12	16
20	8	11	14
25	6	9	11

POST-2008

Businesses saw a double change from 2008, with writing-down periods for routine purchases on which allowances reduced from 25 per cent to 20 per cent rising from 9 to 11 years (using 90 per cent of the expenditure as a basis), but the period reducing for "long life" assets and the new integral features reducing from 38 years to 22 years as a result of the rise in rate from 6 per cent to 10 per cent.

2012

Businesses will now see the period over which tax relief is given rise for both classes of asset from 11 years to 12 years for most asset purchases, and from 22 to 28 years for long-life assets and integral features.

All in all, this seems a moderate way to finance a reduction in the rate of corporation tax – even if businesses do not consider that they have much to gain from the reduction in rates, there seems little doubt that a reduction was necessary as a competitive measure, to keep the UK aligned or no worse than comparative rates through the EU.

As part of the material produced on Budget Day, the Government released a document titled "Tax policy making: a new approach". This discussion document set out a number of proposals for improving the framework for developing, legislating and implementing tax policy. The Government is planning to meet interested parties to discuss its overall approach over the next financial year (2010/11) to discuss these areas of interest and concern.

It was also confirmed that the Government proposes to consult on reforms in a number of areas, including:

- corporation tax reform – a business forum will be established, chaired by the Exchequer Secretary to the Treasury, to look into corporation tax reform and tax competitiveness in the UK;
- controlled foreign companies (Summer 2010) – on interim improvements to the rules to be legislated in Spring 2011. New rules are to be introduced in Spring 2012;
- taxation of foreign branches (Summer 2010) – looking at a move to a more territorial approach;
- taxation of intellectual property – research and development tax credits and the proposals from the Dyson Review;
- taxation of non-domiciled individuals – to consider whether changes can be made to ensure that a fair contribution is made to reducing the deficit;

- PAYE – to consider how the system could be made easier to operate for employers;
- pensions – to consider the requirement to purchase an annuity at the age of 75 and to reform the existing tax allowances;
- climate change levy;
- general anti-avoidance rule – an examination as to the need, long debated, for an overarching rule to prevent avoidance of tax;
- IHT on trusts – should this area be brought within the "disclosure of tax avoidance schemes" regime?;
- banking remuneration disclosure scheme;
- EU cost-sharing exemption – whether it should be implemented in the UK.

INDEX